WILL YOU READ ME A STORY?

The Parent's Guide to Children's Books

Tony Bradman

THORSONS PUBLISHING GROUP
Wellingborough, Northamptonshire
———•———
Rochester, Vermont

First published 1986

© TONY BRADMAN 1986

British Library Cataloguing in Publication Data

Bradman, Tony
Will you read me a story? : the parent's
guide to children's books.
1. Children's literature   2. Book selection
I. Title
028.5′34   Z1037.A1

ISBN 0-7225-1271-6

Cover illustrations from *Bedtime*
© by Helen Oxenbury (Walker Books)

Printed and bound in Great Britain

WILL YOU READ ME A STORY?

Leabharlanna Poiblí Átha Cliath
Dublin Public Libraries

Invaluable advice, from a parent *for* parents, on making
the most of books with your children, from their earliest
days onwards.

For Emma, Helen and Thomas –
the best kids of all

Contents

Acknowledgements

The debts I owe to all the people I've met and talked to during the years in which I've been involved in children's books are enormous. It goes without saying that there are far too many friends, colleagues, helpers and acquaintances to mention by name. And as I've learned from my children, if you can't mention them all, it's wiser not to mention any of them. So thanks to everyone who's helped me learn about children's books.

But the biggest thanks must go, as usual, to my children, who really did teach me what I know about children's books – it's their distilled wisdom in the pages which follow – and most of all to Sally, who continues to put up with someone who is much less than Prince Charming, especially when he's writing a book. Without her love and support this book would not exist at all.

Thanks to the following publishers, who have permitted the use of copyright material in the illustrations: Andersen Press, London, for *Not Now Bernard* © by David McKee; Blackie and Son Ltd, Glasgow, for the *Topsy and Tim* books © Jean and Gareth Adamson; The Bodley Head, London, for *Chips and Jessie* © by Shirley Hughes, *I Want to See the Moon* © by Louis Baum and illustrated by Niki Daly, *In the Night Kitchen* ©by Maurice Sendak; Jonathan Cape Ltd, London, for *Mister Magnolia* © by Quentin Blake, *The Twits* © by Roald Dahl and illustrated by Quentin Blake; Kestrel Books, London, for *The Baby's Catalogue* © by Janet and Allan Ahlberg; Julia MacRae Books, London, for *Gorilla* © by Anthony Browne; Methuen Books Ltd, London, for *Daisy and the Baby Sitter* © by Tony Bradman and Priscilla Lamont; Piccadilly Press, London, for *The Bad Babies' Counting Book* © Tony Bradman and illustrated by Debbie van der Beek; Walker Books Limited, London, for *Bedtime*, *Friends* and *Working*

© by Helen Oxenbury, *When We Went to the Park* © by Shirley Hughes.

Foreword

I've heard it said many times by booksellers and publishers that many parents would rather spend five or six pounds on the latest craze toy than a few pounds on a book. It's a fact I find very depressing and I am constantly trying to convince parents that books are one of the best investments they can make for their children's future.

Early literacy and a keen interest in written materials are of vital importance to children if they are going to grow up to enjoy learning and gathering knowledge. No matter how advanced we become technologically there is no substitute for a book both as a source of knowledge and entertainment. Since my little boy Aston was a tiny baby he has had books all around him and it always gives me and my husband great pleasure to watch him go to his own special bookshelf when he wants to find out something or choose a book he wants to read a story from.

Books are where children learn about the world that surrounds them and it's from the examples they see in books that their opinions and beliefs are formed. So it's essential for parents to choose books that accurately reflect the society in which we live.

In this book Tony Bradman gives parents a crash course in getting the best from the thousands of children's books available in bookshops today. How to choose them, and how to use them, how to find them, and which ones to buy.

If you are daunted, as many parents are, by the mind-boggling choice of children's books available today – some good, others not so good – then this is the book you should start with. It will be a sound investment for you and your children.

Floella Benjamin

Introduction

I nearly didn't write this book. In fact, when it was suggested to me that I should, I wasn't at all sure it was a good idea. A guide to children's books? Hasn't it already been done?

Of course it has, and more than once. There are several other books which could be gathered together under that heading. I would even go so far as to say that two of them – Dorothy Butler's *Babies Need Books* and Jim Trelease's *The Read-Aloud Handbook* – are essential reading for *all* parents.

So why *did* I write this book? The reason is simple. I believe that our children's minds and lives can be enriched enormously if we provide them with good children's books. But that simple belief can be very hard to put into practice. It's all very well to say that our children need books but, as a parent, where do you start? What should you look for in a children's book? How can you tell whether a particular book will suit your child when she's two, or five, or eight? How can you afford the books? Where do you get hold of them? And once you've got the books, what's the best way to use them so that your child gets the maximum benefit?

These questions – and others – are the ones that this book is designed to answer. In my experience, they're the questions which worry most parents when the subject of children's books crops up. They're also the questions which Dorothy Butler and Jim Trelease have tried to answer – so what, you might ask, makes my book different?

Much as I admire and respect both *Babies Need Books* and *The Read-Aloud Handbook*, I don't think Dorothy or Jim would ever claim that they've exhausted the subject of children and books. Parents will always need advice about using books with their children. If an idea is worth discussing once, too, surely it's worth discussing it again . . . and again . . . and again . . . and I believe that the ideas I'm dealing with in this book cannot be raised often enough.

Even more importantly, *Will You Read Me A Story* takes a slightly different tack to other books in this field. For example, you won't find long lists of recommended books in what follows. I do talk about individual books, and I have included a short list of books I believe no child should miss out on. However, it's much more important for you to have a general idea of what to look for in a children's book, so that you can make the right decisions for your child when faced by row upon row of books in a shop or library.

It's fine to have a list of books to work from. But there's nothing more frustrating for you – or your child – than to discover that the book on the list you're looking for is no longer available, not stocked by your bookshop, or on loan from the library to somebody else. Every year, too, thousands of new children's books are published, while thousands become unavailable because they've gone out of print. That means that lists of recommended books can go out of date very quickly – sometimes even before they're published.

We parents are very busy people, too, and I know from personal experience that we rarely have the time to sit down and read long books which tell us what we ought to be doing – we're usually too busy getting on with family life! In fact, while I've been writing this book I've often had to break off to deal with some of the everyday crises, both major and minor, of life with small children. I've also had to stop writing from time to time to satisfy my children's seemingly endless need to be read to. So I'll quite understand if you have to keep breaking off from reading this to change nappies, stop saucepans boiling over, get babies off to sleep and older children off to school, and generally get on with the 24-hour-a-day job that is parenthood. That's why, among other things, you'll find a section further on about how to fit reading books to your children into a very busy life!

So what exactly is this book all about? It's designed to be a basic guide to finding out about children's books and how to use them.

In *Part 1*, it will tell you why children's books are important, and what they'll do for your child – and for you. In *Part 2* it will talk about what sorts of books are best for your children at different ages and stages. In *Part 3* it will explain what to look for when choosing books, and how to use them. In *Part 4* it will tell you where to get hold of books, how to get more for your money, and where to get further information about children and reading. And in *Part 5* I've put together that list of books no child should miss, that I've already mentioned.

As far as age ranges are concerned, this book is written for anyone who is interested in children and books, but will probably be of most use to parents of young children – that is, babies, toddlers, pre-schoolers and early readers. That covers children from birth to, roughly, the age of seven or eight. To be honest, that's partly because I have personal experience of using books with children under eight – so far. But it's also because those years are very important.

Indeed, if you can get your child interested in books when she's a baby or a toddler, then there's a strong likelihood that she'll stay interested through her childhood and beyond, with your help. Of course, parents of older children still need advice and information about their children's reading and children's books. But as I'm beginning to find out with my own kids, once they're really into books they begin to make their own decisions. It doesn't take much to make books and reading a vital and natural part of your children's lives – and a natural part of family life. Although that will only happen if you're sure it's worth doing – and that's something I hope to convince you of in what follows.

1

What's so special about books?

I sometimes think that people take children's books a little too seriously. Of course I believe that they're important – I wouldn't be writing this book if I didn't. But it's still worth keeping the subject in perspective.

Children do need books, but they certainly don't need them in the way that they need food, warmth, somewhere to live, security and love. Children who have to do without any of these things, or who don't get enough of them, suffer greatly. Children who aren't given books, and who aren't read to or encouraged to read, do miss out on a great deal. But it is possible to grow up to be healthy, happy and normal even if you come into contact with very few children's books at all.

People often link books and education. It's sometimes thought that there's a connection between giving a child lots of books and their achieving 'success' at school. Children who have learned to use and enjoy books from an early age certainly do tend to have some advantages at school. But giving your child a lot of children's books is no guarantee that she will be any more of a success than she would otherwise have been. How your child gets on at school depends on many factors; her natural talents, abilities and interests, your support and interest, how good the school is and what sort of resources it has, what the teachers are like . . . and so on. Of course, books can and do play a vital part in your child's education – but they're not the be all and end all.

It's important to bear in mind, too, that books are only one of a number of options open to our children for information and entertainment these days. Our children can watch television instead of looking at books. They can use video machines to increase the variety of things they watch on TV. They can play games on their personal computers, listen to stories on tape cassette or read comics. Books have got to compete with all these other very attractive forms of entertainment as well as older, more traditional forms of play, for our children's attention and interest.

It's very easy to look down on things like televison and comics. Actually, I think that there are many very good things to be seen on the small screen, especially in children's programming. However, there's also a lot of rubbish, and it's important not to allow your children to become televison addicts, or to let them watch programmes which are not intended for them. But there's no need to throw the baby out with the bathwater, as it were. Television is not going to go away, and few families are prepared to take drastic action and give up television altogether. But it can be controlled and, if it is, it can be an enjoyable and useful part of family life. It can even get your children interested in books, among other things!

So what is it that books can offer your children? Of all the options open to them I believe that books represent the best value. That's because books don't just do one thing; they do almost as many things as there are individual titles. Books can entertain, inform, instruct; they can teach you about other people and yourself. They can stimulate your imagination and help you learn about living. Books can actually help your children in that most difficult of tasks, growing up. Books can do so many different things that it's almost impossible to generalize about them. So, in the rest of this section, I'm going to look at some of the specific things they can do.

Fun, fun, fun

One of the biggest attractions of children's books – and of books in general – is that they can be a lot of *fun*. Children like to laugh; it's one of the nicest things about them. They like to laugh from the time they're small babies onwards, and there is nothing so satisfying for a parent than to do something which brings out those wonderful whoops of glee and childish giggles. But you can't tickle your toddler all day long, and few of us can keep up a constant stream of jokes or funny faces. That's where children's books come in.

There are so many good children's books around, too, that you should never be short of a book to make you and your children laugh. There are board books with funny pictures for babies, pop-up and novelty books which do outrageously funny things, hilarious picture books and longer stories which will keep beginner readers in stitches. When I've talked to parents who have begun to find out about the wealth of good children's books available today, one of the commonest things I've heard them say is that they didn't realize books could be so much fun.

This is a point I can't stress enough. If you're looking for a way of keeping your children happy and entertained, a way of putting some joy into their lives, then children's books can't be bettered. They'll give you a few laughs, too, and that's something we all need from time to time. Parenthood can occasionally be a pretty stressful occupation, and humour is a great help in coping with the stresses and strains of life with small children. I've often found that, after a hard day, reading a funny children's book to my kids can really chase the blues away. And if it's a story about a grumpy dad who's been working too hard, then it can even help to put a few things into a new perspective!

Family life

That last point is an example of the way in which children's books can make a positive contribution to family life. If your children enjoy books, then there will always be something for them to do. A small pile of books is an excellent way of easing the boredom of a long journey by train, bus, car or plane, for instance. It's no guarantee that they won't get bored or fractious and end up misbehaving but, so long as it doesn't make your children feel travel sick, looking at books will certainly help to keep them occupied and quiet for a time – so it's always worth a try.

You can also use books to help you cope when your child is feeling unwell. It's at those times when a child is feeling ill enough not to want to play much, but is well enough to be awkward, that a few good children's books are worth their weight in gold. And, of course, there are always those days when it's raining, and there's nothing interesting on television and your child is bored with all her toys. Books can help to fill those voids, too, and sometimes save you from being whined at by your kids.

Something else I've discovered is that a child who has been brought up on books soon learns to entertain him or herself from time to time. Even at the age of just one, my son Thomas could often be seen deeply engrossed in a picture book or tugging away at a flap in a pop-up. At times he really does keep himself occupied and out of our hair for ten minutes or more in this way. It might not sound long but if you've got small children you'll know how blissful it can be to have ten minutes to yourself sometimes!

It's also been a delight for me to see how books have helped to build relationships between my children. Of course they argue a lot, as all small children do with their brothers and sisters, and sometimes those arguments are over who gets to have what book. But every so often I come across seven-year-old Emma reading to five-year-old Helen and two-year-old Thomas, or Helen enjoying a pop-up book with her younger brother. It's enough to warm the heart of an old softie like me, and I usually feel quite emotional – until one of them turns round and belts the other!

We're lucky now in that Emma has reached the stage where she can read to herself and the others when she feels like it, and it won't be long before Helen's in the same position. But before your children learn to read, it's you who has to do the reading, although there are quite a number of wordless books which babies, toddlers and even older children can enjoy looking at on their own. But those family reading sessions do have benefits in themselves.

In *Babies Need Books*, Dorothy Butler explains very well that reading books with your baby or toddler is as important a physical and emotional experience as it is an 'intellectual' one. Your baby enjoys receiving plenty of attention from you, and that's what she feels she's getting when you sit her on your lap to look at a picture book together.

The close physical contact, your voice telling a familiar funny or interesting story, the quiet concentration on the pictures or the laughter stimulated by the book, all combine to give your child the sort of reassuring, positive experience which builds up her sense of security, of being loved and valued. Those feelings will only be strengthened if you give your child that sort of experience regularly throughout her early childhood.

The value of your reading sessions can grow as your children get older. Having a regular story time each day lets your child know that, whatever else happens, she can count on your undivided attention for at least twenty minutes or half an hour, or even longer if she's lucky. Life with small children can be very hectic. It sometimes seems as if it's nothing but an endless round of meals, wiping noses, clearing up and telling off. Reading books to your children can be a way of spending time with them that's positive and enjoyable. That can only help to strengthen the relationship between you, especially if story time involves having fun, too.

We're like many families in that our main reading sessions happen at the children's bedtime every night. Those quiet half hours, which sometimes stretch to an hour or more, are very precious to us. For a little while we can forget our troubles and spend some time together having a few laughs. Sometimes the children misbehave (the most common source of argument being who gets to choose the next book), and sometimes I'm grumpy or tired. But for the most part we all enjoy those story sessions, and feel refreshed because of them. It's a marvellous way to end the day, and beats watching TV by a long way.

Often I find that, simply because we're spending some time quietly together, my children and I end up talking about things which might be on our minds – problems at school, things which might have been worrying them and so on. It might be the story we're reading which sparks off the discussion but, whatever it is, I find out a lot about what's going on in their lives and minds – and that's very important. Those reading sessions are periods of communication between us, and in these days when there is so much pressure on young families, such time spent together can be very valuable indeed.

It's certainly very valuable for fathers, especially. If you're a dad

He has an old trumpet
that goes rooty-toot —

From Mr Magnolia *by Quentin Blake (Cape and Fontana).*

who is the family's main breadwinner, and who spends most of his day out of the home and away from his kids, an evening reading session can be an excellent way of bringing you and your children together. Some dads feel a little 'left out' of family life, and wonder how they can become part of their children's lives in a positive, valuable way. Making the effort to read to your children can be a real help.

Reading books at bedtime can have a very direct and practical effect on your children, too. Early evening is often the toughest time for parents of small children, and reading books with your kids can have a very calming and relaxing effect on boisterous children who might otherwise want to continue racing around the house creating mayhem until all hours. It can be very calming for overwrought parents, too, and there are many of us who have quietly dozed off in the middle of *Cinderella* or *Topsy and Tim Go on Holiday*, much to the disgust of a child who's eager to finish the story.

Books can, therefore, be a vital and rewarding part of family life. Favourite books and favourite characters from stories have almost become a part of our family. The books we've read together have become entangled with memories of particular times and events. They've become part of our common stock of images and examples. If a doll loses a shoe, then it might not be so bad, because she's like Quentin Blake's *Mr Magnolia* who only had one boot; if I walk into a door because I'm not looking where I'm going my kids take great delight in telling me I'm like *Willy the Wimp*, in Anthony Browne's book of the same name, who walks into a lamp post.

I have to admit that there are times when books can be *too* prominent a part of family life. Sometimes my heart sinks and my eyes glaze over with boredom when Helen or Thomas ask me to read, for the umpteenth time, the dullest book they've got. And sometimes I'm too tired or preoccupied to read to my children, which is a disappointment for them and makes me feel guilty. These are problems I'll be looking at further on, but it's enough here to say that we all feel like that from time to time. None of us is perfect, after all!

Books and your child's development

Books can make some very much more specific contributions to your child's development. In recent years there has been a positive flood of books designed to help your child by exploring special situations or stages of development. I'm talking about books which deal with starting playgroup or going to school, books about wetting the bed, having nits, coping with the arrival of a new baby brother or sister, being adopted, or the death of a favourite pet. The range of such titles is enormous, and it sometimes seems to me that there is hardly a 'special situation' in family life which isn't covered by at least two or three children's books.

I have to say that often such books are very dull simply because they tend to be very earnest and sincere. They're also very blunt instruments when it comes to dealing with large and important issues in childhood. I would be the first to admit that even a very well produced, well meaning children's book can at best only play a part in helping your child come to terms with the idea of death, or her jealousy of a baby brother. Such things by their very nature have to be dealt with positively over a period of time in the context of a family which makes a child feel loved, secure and valued.

First she asked for
a drink of water.

Then she asked when Mum
and Dad would come back.

Then she asked
for another drink
of water.

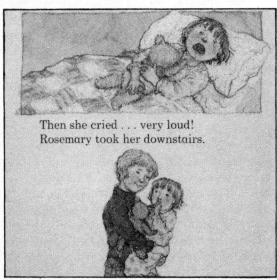

Then she cried . . . very loud!
Rosemary took her downstairs.

From Daisy Tales by Tony Bradman and Priscilla Lamont (Methuen).

Nevertheless, 'special situation books' _can_ play a part at certain times simply because they help to open up a subject. Your own anxiety about the effect of sending your child to playgroup, for example, could make it difficult for you to talk about it. Using a book about playgroup might help, and it will also give you something concrete to talk about – which, for a child, is much better than vague conversations about something she knows little about. I've found that, with certain subjects, my children have found some books so valuable that they've wanted them to be read over and over again.

That's a common reaction. It means that a particular book is speaking to a child directly about something of very great concern, and it's one reason why fairy tales and some of the classic nursery stories have such a powerful effect. If you think about it, the world is a big, scary place for small children. They're very vulnerable – and they know it. What would happen if mother and father weren't around to protect them? How would they survive? Who can they trust, and who should they avoid?

These are the sorts of questions which fairy tales and nursery stories pose – and answer. If your father and stepmother abandon you, as in the story of _Hansel and Gretel_, you survive by being brave and quick-witted. You don't trust The Big Bad Wolf, whether he's outside your house huffing and puffing and trying to blow it down, or inside grandmother's clothes waiting to gobble up you and your Red Riding Hood.

It may seem a large claim to make for such stories, but they do help your children learn about the world, and therefore to begin the process by which they learn how to deal with its problems and dangers. The reason these stories have survived and are still so popular is that they pose the big questions in a safe way. In a sense they're like training exercises which explore things that might worry your child. They don't have to go out into the wild wood and meet strange characters simply to learn the lesson that sometimes people aren't what they seem, and that you need to be careful about strangers. The story of Red Riding Hood tells them that in a memorable way.

It's important, of course, for you to take the time to talk about the issues behind stories like Hansel and Gretel, and in ways which your children can understand. If you do that, then you'll be using children's books and stories in exactly the right way, and you'll help to increase your child's sense of security at the same time. Fairy tales usually have happy endings. The goodies win and the baddies get punished – much to your child's satisfaction. Such stories will tell her that the world can be a dangerous place – but also that she can overcome or avoid the dangers.

Obviously it isn't quite that simple, but the time for doubts and less positive endings to stories will come later as your children grow older and gain more experience of the world. What you will find with young children, however, is that they often make a total, all-enveloping response to the stories you read to them. They immediately relate what they're hearing in the story and seeing in the pictures to their own experience, which is why you sometimes need to be careful about the books you use with your children – a point I'll be returning to further on. So, although a story might seem to you to be silly, trivial or dull – or all three at the same time – often it will go direct to the heart of your children's main concerns. That's why you might find yourself reading the same books to them over and over again.

It isn't just the classic fairy tales which have this quality, either. There are plenty of modern books which do the same, books which will become classics in their turn. Many picture books can in fact be used as 'special situation books' because the story is about going to playgroup or the arrival of a new baby. You can use children's books as a constant source of support for your child as she grows and develops, a way of deepening her understanding of the world she finds herself in.

Don't forget, either, that reading books with your child is an excellent way of finding out what interests and concerns her. If, for example, you find over a period of time that the stories your child returns to again and again involve characters who feel left out or undervalued because of the arrival of a new baby, then that's an important piece of information about her feelings. Many of the best children's books also show great insight into the ways in which children's minds work, and I feel that, through reading books with my children, I've come to understand a little more about children in general.

And perhaps one of the major benefits of children's books for _children_ is that the stories in them often explore relationships between parents and children, or between children themselves, which is something books for grown-ups do, too. It might be hard to think of a story in which the principal characters are small furry animals as doing this – but they do. If Peter Rabbit doesn't get on with his mother, it doesn't matter that he's a small furry animal – what matters to your child is the problem and its solution!

There's one other aspect of your child's development on which reading stories regularly will have a marked and noticeable effect over the years, and that's her speech. I'm not claiming that by reading stories to your child you'll guarantee that she'll learn to talk any more quickly than she would otherwise have done. As with most aspects of your child's development, learning to talk depends on many factors, not the least of which may well be your child's genetic inheritance. Some perfectly normal children of highly articulate, talkative parents simply start talking late, while other kids launch themselves into language much earlier.

Nevertheless, it's clear that the more language your child is exposed to, the sooner and better she's likely to get to grips with speech. Even though your child may be a late talker, and may not start using words until well after children of the same age, she'll still probably understand quite a lot of what you say. She has to understand the language before she can use it, and therefore she needs to hear as much of it as she can.

We all run out of steam in the end though, and not even the most talkative of parents can keep up a stream of language directed at a child all the time. Equally, it's important to vary the diet – which is where the children's books come in. No only do children's books contain ready made language in the form of stories and rhymes, it's language which is often interesting in itself – and fun. It's important to bear in mind the simple fact that children who have a lot of stories read to them do often end up with a better grasp of language and a wider vocabulary.

Books and education

I've begun to talk about learning, and that brings us to the one benefit that we most often associate with children's books – their usefulness in our children's education.

The very idea of 'learning' naturally calls up an image of books and, even in this age of computers and videos, much of your child's education will involve the use of books. But your child can start learning from books long before she gets to school. Even books for the very young can broaden a child's experience and introduce her to things she has never encountered before and might not otherwise meet.

My kids had met elephants, parrots and even alligators in children's books long before they ever made their first trip to a zoo, and there are many, many other things children will come across in the stories you read to them. In this sense you lay the foundations to your children's understanding of books as sources of information, tools they can use to find out about the world around them. A toddler who looks at a board book with pictures of animals or everyday objects in it is engaged in an activity very similar to the college student using her textbooks or an encyclopaedia. The difference is only one of level.

You might feel that your child could get plenty of information and learn about the world from some of the excellent television programmes broadcast these days. That's true, but there are few programmes that go into the depth a good book can, and the point of using books with small children is to get them used to the idea, so that they'll understand this aspect of books and be able to use them as resources when they're older. Besides, books can enormously extend your child's necessarily limited opportunities for new experience whether she watches much TV or not.

There are other 'educational' benefits to books as well. One very basic advantage you'll be giving your children by reading to them regularly is that you'll help to develop their powers of concentration. Children who can concentrate have a head start when it comes to doing school work; indeed, it's probably one of the most important abilities your child can gain. The experience of being read to, of following a story in words and pictures, is essential in this respect, and the more you read to your children, the better it will be for their powers of concentration – especially if the stories are interesting!

Regular reading sessions will also help to make your children familiar with the strange conventions of books – things such as always starting at one end of a book and going through it to the other end, following the story through the pictures and words. Remember, it isn't obvious to your child that you read what's on one page and _then_ turn to the next, or that you read lines of print from left to right, and go back to the left to start each new line!

You'll help your child understand that point, for example, simply by running your finger under the words as you read the story. By doing so you'll also help her to learn one of the most important lessons in her life, which is that the words we speak can be written down, and that once they're written down they don't change. In a sense, it will be like magic to your child at first – every time you open a book and read a story you read it in exactly the same way. It won't be all that long before your child begins to connect the black squiggles on the page with the words that come out of your mouth – and that's an amazing leap of the understanding.

Indeed, even wordless picture books for the very young can play their part in helping your child in this respect. In the best books, the pictures are an essential part of the flow of the story, either telling it themselves or working with the words to put it across. The _idea_ of story is important in itself, too. It involves a sequence of events happening one after the other, of actions causing other actions or being the results of what happens. None of these things are totally obvious to your child, but they're important lessons which can be learnt very simply through children's books.

That's why I think you should consider reading stories to your child in the very early years, as an essential preparation for her formal education. You're laying the foundations on which your child's teachers – with your help, participation and co-operation – will build. On a very simple level, making books part of your child's pre-school life will ensure that they won't come as something of a shock when he enters the classroom – and that has to be a major educational advantage.

Going to school without any knowledge of books is like being asked to build a house with no knowledge of bricks, or wood, or cement or any of the tools that you need. Knowing about books puts your child in the position of someone who at least knows how to use the tools to do the job, even though she's going to need lots of help to get it finished. for the child who's been read to regularly, books are old, familiar friends.

Nowhere is this more important than in the process of learning to read, something many parents worry about these days. You might wonder how you can help your child to learn to read, and the simple answer – as you might have guessed by now – is just to read to your children as much as possible. You can play a vital part in helping your child learn to read simply by getting her interested in books. It's always easier to learn to do anything if we're interested in it, and keen to succeed, and you can foster that sort of attitude in your children just by making books and reading fun, exciting and a natural part of family life.

The idea of books as fun brings me back to where I started, and it's a point I can't emphasize enough. Often, in our concern for our children to do well at school, we can give them the impression that books are terribly important, and therefore very serious. But I always try to remember that the quickest way to a child's heart is through fun.

Imagination

Children's books do something else, too, something I can only describe in a phrase which is almost a cliché – they stimulate your child's imagination. Of course books are important in education, and children need to know that they're sources of information. But for me, the most important thing about books is that they tell stories, stories about real life, or dragons and fairies, the past or the future. The delight that a well-written, well-illustrated story can give your child is of value *in itself*, and the more stories your child experiences, the richer will her imagination be. That sort of enrichment will simply make your child's life fuller and better than it would otherwise have been.

You can see just how important that enrichment is by the sort of response your child will make to books, given half the chance. It's always amazing to me to see a child who was running about creating mayhem ten minutes before sitting quietly, totally absorbed in the story that's being read. Given the best children's books, your children will sometimes happily spend reading sessions in rapt concentration and delight.

Helping your child to find that sort of pleasure and stimulation in books is, as far as I'm concerned, one of the most constructive and positive things you can do as a parent. By reading your children stories you are giving them one of the most valuable experiences known to the human race. It would be marvellous, in fact, if _all_ our children had access to all the books they needed and could feel that books were a natural part of living. Then people like me wouldn't have to spend their time writing books like this, and we could use the time instead to read more stories to our own children!

2

Which books are right for my child?

As a proud – and very bookish – new father, I was keen that my first child should have plenty of children's books. So one day, when Emma was about six months old, I strapped her into the buggy and set off for a bookshop. What could be simpler or more pleasant, I thought, than to spend a Saturday afternoon choosing a few books for my daughter and I to enjoy together?

Problem number one came when we arrived at the bookshop, where I soon discovered that it was almost impossible with the pushchair to get up the two steps to the shop entrance and open the door. I managed it in the end by dint of lots of pushing and shoving, and eventually I flew into the shop feeling very conspicuous. Problem number two came when Emma decided that the massed ranks of brightly coloured paperbacks on low shelves were far too tempting for a six month old to resist, and proceeded to remove them by the dozen. Problem number three came when she objected strongly – and very loudly – to having a chewed paperback removed from her possession, and problem number four came soon after, when she filled her nappy. Isn't shopping with a baby in a pushchair a delight?

Problem number five, however, the biggest problem of all, had nothing to do with Emma. It was my own complete ignorance of children's books, which meant that I had virtually no idea of which books were suitable for Emma at her stage. I remember wandering round this well-stocked, highly respected children's bookshop in a daze. I picked up books, looked at them, looked at Emma, and wondered whether they were right. Many of them looked terrific. Most of them seemed terrifically expensive, and I was worried that if I bought the wrong books they would be a waste of money. And as we were in the same financial situation as most young families – that is, desperate, or slightly worse – that was something I wanted to avoid at all costs (I apologize for the pun).

On subsequent visits to the same bookshop I found some of the staff very helpful indeed. But on that particular Saturday afternoon, near Christmas, the shop was very crowded and the staff were obviously terribly busy, so there was no one available who could tell me which of the wonderful books I was looking at would be suitable for my child. So I struggled with my wailing baby through crowds of toddlers and harrassed parents, and emerged at last with several books I was unsure about and a cheque stub on which a worryingly large figure was scribbled. Alas, none of the books I had bought proved to be all that popular at home. In fact, I read them to Emma a couple of times without much response, and then quietly put them on the shelf, never to be looked at again.

Had I been less determined to make sure that my daughter should be given the chance to enjoy books, I might have given up there and then. It wasn't just the cost, either, that was the problem. I was as bewildered by the choice of books in the library when I took Emma there for the first time, too. I struggled on, however, continuing to fork out cash for books I wasn't sure about. Gradually I began to find out about children's books – but I did it the hard way.

That's why in this section I'm going to outline the stages of your child's development, and talk about the sorts of books which she will be able to enjoy at each stage. If you want to ensure that your child gets the best out of children's books, then she needs to have the right books at the right time. It's no use, for example, giving a toddler a book which is designed for a seven or eight year old. That's just confusing and off-putting for her. And a seven year old will quickly get bored with books that are too young for her.

It isn't possible to be rigid about age ranges in children's books, however. As you'll see, the categories are very broad and there is a lot of overlap. Some children can cope with books that seem much too old for them, and in any case it's always worth trying to stretch their 'reading stamina'. At the same time, older children often have favourite books which they will return to again and again, long after they've moved on to much more sophisticated reading matter.

You might think that life would be much simpler for the parent in search of a book for a specific child if publishers put definite age ranges on their products. Some do, but most publishers are wary of being too specific. That's understandable; would you buy a book that said 'suitable for five year olds' if your child was four or six? That book might be right for a broad range of children, anyway, from the bright three year old to a seven year old who just likes that particular type of story.

What this means is that, in general, when publishers *do* put age ranges on books – which isn't very often – they can be so general and vague as to be of little real use, although it's worth checking to see if the publisher is brave or foolhardy enough to have suggested an age range for a book. The best children's bookshop these days also have clearly defined sections for baby books, books for beginner readers and so on, but these bookshops are still too few and far between.

As your children grow, and you use more and more books with them, you'll begin to understand their reading needs, their tastes and their preferences. Eventually you'll probably get to the stage where you can gauge a book's suitability for your child almost at a glance. But you need a good basis on which to start, a set of rough guidelines which will make the beginning of that process of learning as easy as possible.

I've divided what follows, therefore, into four sections. **Books for babies** looks at children from birth to around eighteen months; **Books for toddlers** at children from around eighteen months to around three years; **Books for pre-schoolers** at children from around three to about five years; and **Books for beginner readers** at children from around five to eight. Remember that there's an enormous amount of overlap between these categories, especially the first two. In any one reading session, a child of three or four, for example, might enjoy books from all the categories I'm going to outline. Nevertheless, these four stages do represent a handy way of breaking down the vast range of children's books into something a little easier to manage.

Books for babies

You might think that when your baby is born she isn't capable of very much. In one sense that's true. She certainly can't communicate with you very well, other than to signal her hunger by crying and her contentment by going to sleep. She doesn't have much control over her body, either.

She is, however, capable of more than just crying and sleeping. She can focus her eyes, for instance, although only on objects that are about eight to fifteen inches from her face – which is, interestingly enough, the distance your face is likely to be from hers during feeding, whether by breast or bottle.

Everything is new for her, of course, and in her early days and weeks she may find her surroundings a little confusing, to say the least. All her senses, not just her eyesight, are in full working order, and she soon discovers that life outside the womb is very stimulating indeed. She's bombarded with new sensations, new sounds, new smells, new sights. It's hardly surprising that it takes a little time for her to begin to make sense of what's going on.

Gradually, however, she begins to gain more and more control of her body, a process which takes place from the head downwards. It isn't long before she can hold her head up, and towards the end of her first year she's probably capable of sitting up and may even be crawling round the furniture. By the age of one year she might be standing and taking a few steps with your help, and by the middle of her second year she may well be a proper toddler.

At the same time she will have made great strides in other areas of her development. She will have learned to use her hands in co-ordination with her eyes in her early months, and by the time she's crawling and beginning to walk she will have become very skillful at handling and manipulating objects, although she'll still have a long way to go. As these skills develop, and as she widens the scope of her explorations, she will have more and more opportunity to satisfy one of her main needs – her curiosity, her burning desire to find out about the fascinating world around her.

It's important to remember that your baby really _is_ interested in what's around her. She isn't just a blank slate waiting to be written on by her experiences. She's actively curious, and very keen to find out what that interesting coloured object is, or what happens when you pull this or push that. Visual stimulation is very important to her throughout babyhood too, and one thing she'll be more interested in than almost anything else in her early months is you. That's because you're a major and very important part of her world.

You're her source of food, of comfort and quite often her most amazing and interesting plaything. You're her physical and emotional base, the point at which she starts her explorations of the world. At the beginning, and almost throughout her babyhood, she'll find it hard to be separated from you for long periods unless she's asleep. Independence grows slowly, and is only relative. A fully weaned, active toddler of fifteen months might seem very independent, but she still needs to know that there's a loving adult or two fairly close at hand.

Few children will have started to talk much before the middle of their second year, but language and communication plays a very large part in babyhood. Parents instinctively talk to their babies right from birth, and in a special way, too. You've probably heard yourself doing it; you pitch your voice a little higher than usual, repeat what you say, and use plenty of expression. We all do this, for a very simple reason. Such speech patterns are designed to make it easier for your child to understand that the sounds coming out of your mouth are special, that they mean something. It's also simply more fun for your child! It isn't long before your three or four month old baby is actually taking a part in these 'conversations', by imitating your expressions, sticking her tongue out and making all the noises she can. By the age of a year she may have spoken her first word or two, and will certainly understand much of what you say. During her second year her grasp of – and interest in – language will continue to grow.

Your baby's talents and interests are reflected in the sorts of books that are available for the youngest readers. There are **board books**, for example, small books with stiff pages which are just the right size for your baby's hands. Some of these feature photographs of familiar objects or animals, while others – like the

Two of Helen Oxenbury's hugely popular Baby Board Books *(Walker).*

enormously successful *Baby Board Books* by Helen Oxenbury – feature illustrations of the same sorts of things, with a dash of humour in the presentation of babies and their families. Your baby will respond with pleasure from a very early age – probably from two or three months onwards – to bright, bold pictures of things which she can recognize.

Don't just concentrate on board books, however. There are many picture books which your baby will enjoy, especially if the illustrations are bright and colourful, as they are in Dick Bruna's bold, simple books for babies. And don't think that babies don't appreciate a book with words; they will. Obviously the text in a book for a baby needs to be short and to feature words which aren't too difficult. It also helps if the words have rhythm and maybe even rhyme. The best sort of text for babies is a nursery rhyme, and there are numerous bright, bold books based on individual rhymes, such as the *Jollypops* books by Colin and Jacqui Hawkins. As you baby gets older and gains more of a grasp of language he'll be able to cope with longer stories, and you'd be surprised just how many words an eighteen-month-old is prepared to sit and listen to!

There are also plenty of books which fall into the 'gimmick' or 'novelty book' category. I'm talking about the large number of pop-up and lift-the-flap books which are now available, many of which young babies adore. All my children have loved Eric Hill's Spot books, for example, and we're now on our third copy of Robert Crowther's *Most Amazing Hide-and-Seek Alphabet Book*, the book in which all sorts of animals are made to appear from behind their own initial letters. Babies can be a bit heavy on books, especially books like these. But that's no reason not to give them to your baby, and the delight they can give makes the effort to protect them worthwhile.

In fact it's worth keeping a supply of magazines, old catalogues, comics and any old pictures around too. Your baby can be safely destructive with these, which might help to protect her books! Most babies love looking at pictures, and it won't be long before they start recognizing cars, cats and hosts of other things in what they see. Indeed, one excellent book for babies is *The Baby's*

A typically humorous page from The Baby's Catalogue *by Janet and Allan Ahlberg (Viking Kestrel and Puffin).*

Catalogue by Janet and Allan Ahlberg, a picture book which simply features illustrations of different families with babies doing everyday things, and plenty of objects that will be interesting and familiar to your baby, from highchairs to toys and potties. _The Baby's Catalogue_ was one of baby Thomas Bradman's all time favourite books, although he also enjoyed really getting his teeth into more ordinary catalogues and magazines.

Babyhood of course is the time for nursery rhymes, songs and games like 'This Little Piggy' and 'Ride a Cock Horse'. That's why a couple of collections of rhymes and games are absolutely essential for parents of babies. Like most of us you can probably remember quite a few, but certainly not as many as you'll find in a book like _Round and Round the Garden_, a collection of forty finger rhymes and games put together by Sarah Williams and illustrated by Ian Beck. What's special about this book is that it also includes diagrams which show you how to do the actions to accompany the rhymes.

It's also worth buying a big collection of rhymes such as Raymond Briggs' _Mother Goose_, or Tomie de Paola's collection of the same name. Add a copy of _This Little Puffin_, a paperback which includes lots of rhymes, games and songs, and you'll probably never run out of material for rhyme and play sessions with your baby.

In general, therefore, babies appreciate books which are **bright** and **colourful** and which are **visually stimulating**; books which are **simple** and which feature either the **familiar**, or things in which they're interested (such as animals or people); and which have relatively few words, or no words at all. One ingredient that's important though is a sense of _fun_. Remember, babies love to laugh!

Books for toddlers

Being a toddler can sometimes be difficult, both for the toddler herself and for the people around her. Toddlers are often lovable rogues, angels one moment, devils the next. That's because they're still babies in some ways, but babies who are taking their first major steps on the road to independence.

Their increased mobility is, of course, an important point in this context. Your toddler is even more curious about the world she finds herself in than she was as a baby, partly because she now has more opportunity to come across things which make her curious. In fact, she'll be into everything. She'll open cupboards and pull out the contents; she'll follow cables to electric sockets; she'll climb the stairs the minute your back is turned; she'll find all the things she shouldn't and generally drive you to distraction. If it hasn't been before, then your child's safety should be uppermost in your mind at this stage, although it will sometimes seem hard to keep even just one step ahead of her.

The 'terrible twos' also have a tendency to react badly when they're stoppped from doing something. That's because, at this age, your toddler is beginning to develop a sense of her own identity. She knows very definitely now what she wants. The problem is that, often, what she wants is exactly what she can't have. She might want to put her finger in the electric socket; you obviously don't want her to. Unfortunately, she doesn't yet understand that much of what she wants is dangerous or inappro-priate for her; all she knows is that she wants it and that she wants it *now*. The result for your toddler is a great deal of frustration.

Frustration can generate a lot of anger at any time of life, so it's hardly surprising that toddlers have a tendency to throw tan-trums. Not only does your child have to cope with the frustra-tion, she also has to learn to cope with the power of her own emotions. The strength of your child's tantrums – and a two year old in full voice, with actions to match, can be a pretty amazing sight – is a reflection of what's going on inside her. She is swept along on the tide of her feelings and really doesn't know how to control them.

Children of this age can get locked into a pattern of saying 'no' to everything, and life for you can become a seemingly endless round of confrontations over almost every part of the day. It can mean battles over mealtimes, battles over bathtimes, and battles over battles. Indeed, in recent months we've spent a fair amount of time being shouted at by our own little lovable rogue, who will often deny himself the pleasure of something he wants, simply to indulge his desire to exercise his willpower and say 'no!' as often and as loudly as he can.

At times like this you'll wonder why you ever wanted to become a parent. But there is another side to your toddler which will delight you. Toddlers can be very affectionate, and they're much more part of the family now. You'll soon begin to realize that your baby has developed into a small person with a character – as well as a will – of her own. She'll be someone who has to be considered, whose presence will be felt in almost every activity your family undertakes. You'll find that the relationship between you will become deeper and more complex, and also that your child will begin to develop relationships with other people, too – perhaps with brothers or sisters, or other relatives.

One aspect of toddlers that I've always found particularly appealing has been their obvious pleasure in finding out about the world. Although you'll spend a lot of time making sure that your child's curiosity doesn't lead her into trouble or harm, it's important to help her explore the world as much as possible. Sometimes your toddler's explorations will help you to look at the world in the way she does, as something fresh and new and exciting. It's been a delight to me to watch Thomas staring out of the window at bedtime, night after night, and finally to hear him say 'moon' and point at that small silver globe you and I probably take very much for granted.

Language is, of course, very important at this stage. At eighteen months your toddler may be like Thomas, and may have said nothing at all, although he understood a great deal. But by the age of three it's likely that your child will be a little chatterbox, with quite a wide vocabulary and with a grasp of quite complicated language. It's a fascinating development, and one which in Thomas' case I feel sure has been helped by books. For example, I had read a book called _I Want to See the Moon_ to him many times before he used the word. It's a wonderful book by Louis Baum and Niki Daly about a toddler who wakes up in the night, and who wants to see the moon. The fact that it was his dad who changed his nappy and eventually gave him what he wanted made it especially appropriate for Thomas and me to read

"I know what you want," said Daddy. "you want to see the moon."
"Yes please, I want to see the moon," said Toby.

So they went outside, into the garden, to look at the moon...

From I Want to See the Moon *by Louis Baum and Niki Daly (Bodley Head and Magnet).*

together, and I'm sure that's where his interest in the moon came from in the first place.

Despite all this growing independence, however, it's vital that you shouldn't lose sight of the fact that your toddler is still a baby at heart. She's taking her first steps on the road to maturity, but she hasn't come very far at all – and she's got a very long way to go yet. She'll probably still be in nappies for some time to come, although quite a few children achieve nappy-free days (the nights are a bit harder) at some time during their third year. Your child will still be dependent on you for help with all the practical, day-to-day things like getting washed and dressed. You'll probably have to cut her food up for her too, and even help to spoon it in – so life will still be very busy.

With the help of some good children's books, though, life with a toddler can be very rewarding, even at its busiest. I've already mentioned one picture book, and these really begin to come into their own at this stage. Your toddler's increasing grasp of language means that she'll start to appreciate longer stories, and her greater sophistication will also mean that she can cope with slightly more complicated pictures.

There is a vast range of picture books available, and you'll probably find that the choice is bewildering. But at this stage your priorities should still be to find books which are visually stimulating, but which also feature interesting language. A book like Janet and Allan Ahlberg's *Peepo!*, for example, is one which many babies appreciate, but which is also ideal for the young toddler of around two. It has a repetitive, rhyming text, holes on each spread to peep through to the next page, and tells the story of a day in the life of one baby and his family.

Saying that a book is repetitive, for this age range, is not an adverse criticism. Toddlers love repetition and rhyme; they love a book with a text that rocks along. They love cumulative books, books which allow them to join in with noises, and books with surprises at the end. All of these things combine to make *Mr Gumpy's Motor Car* and *Mr Gumpy's Outing* ideal for your toddler. All the animals and a boy and girl pile into Mr Gumpy's boat, for example – and misbehave, as you would expect. The ending is inevitable, but toddlers love a big splash whether they can see it coming or not.

Bad behaviour is a very popular subject with children of all ages, but it's particularly exciting for a tantrum-prone toddler (and sometimes they *are* prone when they're having a tantrum!) to see somebody else being bad in a book. That's why a book like *The Elephant and the Bad Baby* by Elfrida Vipont and Raymond Briggs is so popular – the bad baby in that never, ever says *please*! Any books which feature small children having tantrums are usually very popular with toddlers too.

A favourite with Thomas is *Where the Wild Things Are* by Maurice Sendak. It's about Max, a little boy who's so bad his mother calls him a wild thing and sends him off to bed without his supper. His anger takes him to a land of monsters whom he quells simply with the force of his personality – something which Thomas finds very impressive.

Books which feature stories about family life become increasingly interesting to toddlers as they grow older. Shirley Hughes

Two big girls licking ice-creams,

From When We Went to the Park *by Shirley Hughes (Walker).*

has produced some wonderful books for just this age range in her *Nursery Collection*, and many of her other books are ideal for toddlers – I'm thinking of both *Lucy and Tom* and her *Alfie* books, although their appeal will remain strong for children up to five and even beyond. Picture books by Eve Rice such as *Oh Lewis* and *Goodnight, Goodnight* have also struck a chord with Thomas and are worth looking out for.

Don't forget your nursery rhymes at this stage, either. Toddlers will still love a rhyme and finger play session, although my children always seem to end one by wanting to jump on my head very hard. Toddlers love rhymes and songs, and you'll probably find that they begin to learn them off by heart at this stage.

Those novelty and gimmick books will also still be just as popular as they ever were, perhaps even more so than during babyhood. Most toddlers are great fans of Spot in Eric Hill's wonderful series of flap books about the little puppy such as *Where's Spot?*, *Spot's First Walk*, *Spot's Birthday Party* and so on. There are also some very simple and colourful Spot plastic books – so you can even read to your toddler in the bath!

Now also is the time to introduce your child to counting and alphabet books, if you haven't done so already. There are many counting books – some in pop-up form, such as Robert Crowther's _The Most Amazing Hide-and-Seek Counting Book_ – and they often feature the sort of cumulative, repetitive text which toddlers enjoy. In my own _The Bad Babies Counting Book_, for example, I tried to give toddlers everything they might want – a rhyming story, toddlers misbehaving and plenty of fun. An alphabet book is useful not for the purpose of teaching your child to read – as a toddler she's still too young for that – but as a way of beginning to get her used to the idea of letters. Besides, many of them feature lots of pictures of interesting things, and some are fun, too – such as Sandra Boynton's _A is for Angry_.

The books that toddlers appreciate, therefore, usually have **more words**, although they'll still be quite simple – at least for younger toddlers. They should still be **visually stimulating**, but **stories** and simple books about children and **family life** will be very popular. Toddlers still enjoy **rhymes** and **games** though, and **novelty books** and **pop-ups** of all sorts should give them lots of fun.

Books for pre-schoolers

At three years old, your child will become part of a group of children for whom a definition has only relatively recently been invented. Describing children between the ages of three and five as 'pre-schoolers' is a reflection of the fact that school does begin to loom very large on the horizon for them at this stage.

They have more in common, however, than such a definition might imply. At three your child has come a long way from babyhood. If she hasn't done so already, she will almost certainly say goodbye to nappies forever during her fourth or fifth year. She'll soon be feeding and dressing herself, although she'll probably still need some help from time to time. But in general you'll see her becoming ever more independent and self sufficient.

Other people – and especially other children– will become interesting and important to your child at this stage. As a toddler she may have been quite happy to play _alongside_ another child; as a pre-schooler she will want to play *with* other children, actively and co-operatively.

That's why so many children of this age group enjoy going to playgroup or nursery school. Apart from being an excellent way of preparing your child for full time play school, playgroup will give her the opportunity to meet other children and enjoy a wider range of play opportunities than you can probably provide for her at home. Her play will in fact take on a new quality and intensity at this stage.

Now is the time when your child will really start to enjoy 'role-playing' games, for example. She'll want to use the pots and pans she used to turn into drums as a toddler to 'make breakfast', like daddy does. She'll sit in an old cardboard box and pretend she's driving the car, like mummy. She'll want to dress up and pretend to be a princess, the doctor, the bus driver or the postman. In short, she'll want to give full rein to her imagination, which will be growing in power day by day.

At playschool your child will be encouraged to use her hands a lot. She'll bring paintings and drawings home, and one thing that she'll probably always be willing to do is to pick up her crayons and pencils and scribble. This is good for her imagination, but it's also a very important part of the process by which she gains the physical skills she'll need when she begins to learn to write properly at school. Indeed, many pre-schoolers learn to write their names and a few other words before they start school – and remember, learning to *write* is an important part of learning to *read*. So make sure your child has plenty of pencils, crayons, paints, brushes and scrap paper.

You'll probably be glad to know, too, that your child will be increasingly less volatile. More of her energy will go into play and other, constructive activities, especially if she goes to some form of playgroup, so she'll have less to expend on throwing tantrums. She is also becoming more rational and amenable to argument as her grasp of language continues to develop and she begins to understand more about the world around her and other people.

Indeed, by the age of five, most children are quite articulate little characters. They may even have become rather *too* talkative

– their curiosity is undimmed, and now they're capable of asking plenty of questions. So be prepared to be continually pestered about all sorts of things, from 'Why does it go dark at night?' to 'Why does it take daddy so long to wake up in the morning?'

Your pre-schooler will also be a bundle of energy. Children of this age take a delight in the exercise of their physical abilities which is a joy to watch. They run, jump, climb and generally throw themselves into everything they do with real passion. I have a very deep admiration for those hardy souls who work as playgroup leaders; twenty or thirty excited pre-schoolers can fill a large church hall with a noise you'd hardly believe.

Pre-school children have another side to them, though. They may no longer look like babies, but there will still be times when they need to feel that they're loved and secure. Making her way in the world outside can be very daunting for a four-year-old, even if her experience of that world is limited to a friendly place like playgroup. At the same time her imagination can be a disturbing force as well as an exciting one. Your child will be able to imagine unpleasant things as well as enjoy using fantasy in her play.

Fears of all sorts are quite common in this age group, as are nightmares, which can be very disturbing for your child. And all that energy can also get your child into trouble sometimes. It can take her over so that, in the excitement of a game, she hardly knows what she's doing, a tendency that's a common cause of misbehaviour. It can also lead to a lot of falls and bumps and bruises!

As far as books for pre-schoolers are concerned, children of this age are capable of – and interested in – longer and longer stories and picture books of increasing complexity. The range of picture books available for this age group is enormous, and you'll find that your child will probably develop an insatiable appetite for them. In which case, she'll love books by Shirley Hughes, such as _Dogger_ (about a lost comfort object) and _Helpers_ (about being looked after when mum has to go out), and _Moving Molly_ (about moving house) and _Sally's Secret_ (about a fantasy game). Look out too for the same author's _Lucy and Tom_ books.

I could list picture books by the dozen, picture books about animals such as the *Peter Rabbit* stories by Beatrix Potter, which many children of this age love, or funny stories we've enjoyed enormously such as *The Seven Wild Washerwomen* by John Yeoman and Quentin Blake. The Ahlbergs also have something for this age range, as you'd expect – there's *Burglar Bill*, a very funny story; and *Funnybones*, one of the most original picture books of recent years. So there's no shortage of material as far as picture books for this age range are concerned!

Stories about children like themselves are always popular with pre-schoolers, which explains why so many children over the years have enjoyed the *My Naughty Little Sister* stories by Dorothy Edwards, several of which have been turned into individual picture books, but which are mostly to be found in longer collections.

These have the added bonus of focusing on the relationship between two sisters – most three to five year olds have younger or older brothers or sisters who loom very large in their lives.

That also helps to explain why a series like the *Topsy and Tim* books is so popular with children. Many parents may groan (either inwardly or outwardly) when they're asked to read *Topsy and Tim at the Dentist* for the umpteenth time, and it has to be said that in comparison with many of the amazing children's books around today *Topsy and Tim* titles are a little mundane. But children find them very reassuring, not least because they explore in a straightforward way many of the major issues which face them at this stage. Topsy and Tim do all the things your pre-schooler does – they go to the dentist, they go to playgroup, they have birthday parties, they misbehave – and everything turns out all right in the end.

Now is the time indeed when your child is ready for all those 'special situation' books about dentists, doctors and hospitals. There are many such books available, and they should go some way to satisfying your pre-schooler's demand for knowledge. It's also worth beginning to look at any books which will help to explain things in a direct, simple way, of which there are quite a few. Books about trains, planes, birds, bees, flowers and animals – they'll all help you to deal with some of those endless questions

A few of the vast range of the ever-popular Topsy and Tim *books (Blackie).*

and lay the foundations for the school work your child will soon be facing. Look out for the inexpensive but well-produced Dinosaur paperbacks, many of them by Althea. These little books come in very handy for explaining all sorts of things to inquisitive pre-schoolers, from *How a Television Programme is Made* to what it's like when you go into hospital.

Above all, your child will be ready now for some folk and fairy tales. These unite two things which are ideal for pre-school children – stimulation for the imagination and exploration of subjects they worry about, but which are hard to bring to the surface. I'm talking about their vulnerability, their awareness that the world around them can be a wicked, as well as a friendly place.

Fairy tales can begin to help your child understand that she needs to be careful in her dealings with people, that she needs to be on her guard at times – and also that protection exists, and that she can learn to look after herself. Fairy tales can also be strong meat, however. So although your child will probably enjoy them, some children find them too frightening – even if only occasionally. It's probably a good idea at this stage to keep to simple tales for the time being.

There are many collections available, but I've found that individual tales told in picture book form are often very popular with pre-schoolers. Errol Le Cain is a magical artist who has produced a number of picture books of this type, such as *The Twelve Dancing Princesses* and *Mrs Fox's Wedding*. I would also recommend *The Fairy Tale Treasury*, illustrated by Raymond Briggs, and the *Helen Oxenbury Book of Nursery Stories*.

Pre-school children will still look for fun from their books, so some of the clever pop-ups – such as *Robot* and *Haunted House* – will undoubtedly give them pleasure. But they're also beginning to enjoy playing with words in the form of remembered and made up rhymes and jokes. Such an interest makes your pre-schooler an ideal audience for poetry of all sorts, and there are a number of collections of poetry for this age range which are worth seeking out.

We've particularly enjoyed two collections edited by Jill Bennett, *Tiny Tim* illustrated by Helen Oxenbury, and *Roger Was* a _Razor Fish_ illustrated by Maureen Roffey. Another favourite is also illustrated by Helen Oxenbury, and features lots of naughty children – _A Child's Book of Manners_, with poems written by Fay Maschler.

Pre-school children will, therefore, enjoy **longer picture books** and stories, as well as **special situation** and **information** books. They'll also appreciate **folk** and **fairy tales** and **poetry**.

Books for beginner readers

For most children, the age of five marks a major watershed in their young lives. Starting school at that age takes them out of home for a large part of the day, five days a week. From now on, other people – teachers and friends – will have an increasing influence on your child, and through her, on family life.

Going to school is a big step for your five-year-old, and it's hardly surprising that she should be a little apprehensive about it. What's amazing is that most children take to it so easily, with a minimum of tears and upset. You'll probably find that you worry more about how she gets on than she does! Nevertheless, school will take most of your child's energy, both physically and emotionally, especially to start with. She's going to need all your support and understanding as she takes on the tasks of coping with other children, her teacher, and all the learning she's got to do.

One major task your child faces is that of learning to read. Some children will already have begun to recognize words by the time they start school, particularly if they have been read to a lot and been encouraged by their parents to draw and 'write', too. At school, however, whatever your child's understanding of the printed word, she'll almost certainly be taught to read by means of a structured approach which involves a 'graded reading scheme'. You'll soon find yourself helping your child to learn 'her words', and following her progress through blue, red, yellow or orange readers, or whatever system the school uses.

Learning to read is the key to your child's education; once she can read fluently for herself, whole new areas of study and interest will open for her as if by magic. So it's no wonder that teachers – and parents – lay such stress on it. Indeed, many parents become quite anxious about their children learning to read, especially if it seems to be taking longer than it should be.

The most important thing to remember, however, is that to a large extent, learning to read is like most other areas of your child's development; she'll learn to read when she's ready to, and not before, just as she learned to walk when the time was right to do so. Some children walk sooner than others, and some learn to read more quickly than other children of their age. And no amount of forcing or pressure would make your child achieve it sooner. Indeed, as far as learning to read is concerned, pressure tends to slow the whole process down.

Unlike learning to walk, however, your child does need to be given the means to read and help to achieve it. It's also true that some children do have specific problems such as dyslexia, for which special help is needed. In recent years a debate has been raging in educational circles about learning to read, too. On the one hand there are those who say, more or less, that graded reading schemes are the only way to teach a child to read. On the other hand are those who say that such schemes are dull and boring, and kill a child's interest in reading at the same time as they teach her the rudiments of the skill itself.

Of course the debate isn't quite so simple as that. But in essence that's what the two main camps stand for. It has to be said that most reading schemes *are* dull, and that teachers who have done without them and simply taught children to read through using lots of wonderful children's books of all sorts have achieved some very good results. The key is *interest*. If your child is helped to realize that by learning to read she unlocks a vast treasure store of fun and excitement, then she'll be very keen to learn to read.

I've seen it with my own children; because they know that books are fun, they've actually been impatient to learn to read. In fact once it had 'clicked' for Emma, as it so often does in a mysterious way, she was unstoppable and read everything she could lay her hands on.

It seems to me that the answer to the debate lies in compromise.

Many teachers find it easier to work with graded reading schemes, and many children like them. There's a real sense of satisfaction in going from book one, to book two, three and four and so on; it can give your child a very real sense of achievement which is important. At the very least it will encourage her to keep going. However, using a reading scheme shouldn't rule out using other, probably more interesting and exciting books in class, and that's exactly what many teachers are doing these days.

Schools are often short of money, though, so providing your child with books outside school takes on an increased importance at this stage. So it's important not to give up your reading sessions. What's vital is that you should show interest in your child's efforts to learn to read, and that you should back it up by providing her with the sorts of books she will appreciate and find interesting.

Children of this age are still as energetic and physical as pre-schoolers, sometimes even more so. Friends of their own age are also becoming more and more important, and you'll find yourself constantly pestered by demands from your child to be allowed to play at the house of one friend or another, or to have someone round to your house instead. At the same time you'll begin to see some true independence in your child.

By the age of seven or eight she may well have made that all-important trip alone to the shop on the corner. She may ask for pocket money, and tell you that her best friend gets twice as much as you're prepared to pay out. She may have begun to form some real opinions on certain subjects like how much television she should watch, what clothes she should wear and when she should go to bed, much of which will be heavily influenced by what her friends say. Children of this age are often the original conformists.

You should bear in mind, however, that your opinionated, conformist five- to eight-year-old, although occasionally grown up enough to begin to think that her parents are a bit dated and sometimes even a bit embarrassing, will still need to run to you for security, love and comfort when things go wrong, just as she did when she was a pre-schooler or even a toddler. Her independence will be growing by leaps and bounds, but at heart she's still a small child who from time to time will find the world a frightening place.

It's at this age, if not before, that you should try to make your child aware of the possibilities of abuse and harm inherent in the adult world. Few parents, indeed, can face sending their seven-year-old even as far as the shop on the corner without plenty of warnings about not accepting lifts from strangers.

Five- to eight-year-olds will still enjoy many of the same picture books they liked as pre-schoolers, although obviously they will be ready for even longer stories. It's at this age that the ratio between words and pictures in your child's books should really begin to swing towards the words end of the scale. At four or five your child will probably still need more pictures than words in her books. By the time she's eight, with your help she could well be reading short or even medium length novels with very few pictures at all.

You'll find that your child will soon begin to pick out words and phrases from the books you read together, if she hasn't done so already. Funny, interesting stories with a large text that's easy to read will therefore be very useful. I've found the *Beginner Books* – the original Dr Seuss books such as *The Cat in the Hat* and *There's a Wocket in My Pocket* – very useful in this respect. They're bright, bold and crazy, with plenty of pace, rhythm, rhyme and fun. They may drive you mad, but your children will love them.

Allan Ahlberg's *Happy Families* series is also very useful. Stories such as *Mrs Plug the Plumber* and *Miss Brick the Builders' Baby* are ideal for children who are just learning to read. Indeed, once your child gets to the stage where she can read, it can give her enormous confidence to read through on her own a short book such as one of these – a task that will be much easier if it's a book she's already very familiar with.

At the same time she'll still want to have longer and more demanding stories read aloud to her. In fact in terms of books, your child at this time will probably develop something of a split personality. She'll be capable of understanding stories far more complicated than the ones she can read for herself, especially if

He was sitting in the hall with his tail tucked neatly round his paws. The tip of it was twitching gently.

You horrible cat!

"If you've eaten Chico, I'll never speak to you again, never!" shouted Chips. Albert looked pained and stalked off into the kitchen.

Then another terrible thought struck Chips. How was he going to tell them all at school what had happened to Chico?

Whatever will Mrs James and all the people at school say ?

They all like Chico a lot. How am I going to tell them he's got eaten ?

BOO HOO !

"He may turn up, I suppose," said Mum wearily. But that wasn't very comforting. In fact, Chips wasn't comforted at all. He wouldn't go to bed. He made such a fuss that he woke Gloria, who started to cry too. When Grandpa came in quite late, he found them all in the kitchen and a terrible commotion going on.

From Chips and Jessie _by Shirley Hughes (Bodley Head)._

The hilarious Twits from the book of the same name by Roald Dahl (Cape and Puffin).

you've read to her regularly over the years. Longer and more complicated fairy tales will be very popular; we've found traditional tales very entertaining, but also enjoyed enormously Terry Jones's original *Fairy Tales*, and a wonderful collection of Indian tales by Madhur Jaffrey, *Seasons of Splendour*.

Modern stories are also very popular with this age group; I'm thinking particularly of Roald Dahl's books. One of our most enjoyable reads – which progressed at the pace of a couple of chapters a night – was Dahl's *Charlie and the Chocolate Factory*. We've also enjoyed *The Twits*, *The BFG* and several others by him. Children of all ages seem to love Roald Dahl's stories, and I must say that I enjoy them too.

Poetry can also be very popular with the five to eights, especially if it's funny. Favourites in our house are Kit Wright, whose *Rabbiting On* and *Hot Dog* are terrific, Spike Milligan, Mike Rosen and Roger McGough. It really is worth looking out for good collections of poetry for children of this age; short snippets of funny verse hit just the right chord. *Please Mrs Butler*, poems about school by Allan Ahlberg, is our favourite collection of all.

The day will come, though, at some time between the ages of five and eight, when your child will begin to read for herself. At this stage your task will become a little more difficult. What she now needs is a supply of books which she can cope with, and which are also interesting enough to keep her going. Remember that if you want to help your child to remain a reader, then now is the crucial time. From now on there will be increasing demands on her time and energy, and it's only with your help that she'll have the impetus to stay interested in books.

There are lots of books around for this age group, although they might not be as easy to find as books for other ages. What you should be looking for to suit your beginner reader is a book which has got a lot of text and a few pictures, but in which the words are probably in quite large print, still. A simple rule of thumb is that as your child gains more confidence as a reader, she'll be able to cope with longer and longer stories in smaller and smaller print.

Books I've found particularly valuable for this age range are _The Great Smile Robbery_, a wonderfully funny book which blends words and pictures into a unique experience. Your children will love characters like Mrs Wobblebottom and Sour Puss. _Linda's Lie_ and _I'm Trying To Tell You_ are both collections of school stories by Bernard Ashley which your child, with her experience of school, will understand and appreciate.

Flat Stanley by Jeff Baxter is also very popular with this age group, as are the _Charlie Moon_ books by Shirley Hughes. _Chips and Jessie_ by the same author, with its mixture of comic strip, story and fun is probably the perfect book for the beginner reader.

Finally, don't forget non-fiction. Your child at this stage is becoming increasingly knowledgable because of her schoolwork, and whole new areas of interest will open up for her. So now is the time to start looking at books about dinosaurs, cars, nature and so on, and maybe even think about investing in a junior encyclopaedia, an atlas, and so on.

Five to eight year old children need books, therefore, that will help them in the task of **learning to read.** Books with which they can cope, but which also **interest** and **stimulate** them. **Fairy tales, poetry, school stories,** all are important – but you need to help your child to remember that books are still **fun.**

3
Using books

I hope by now that I've persuaded you to think of books as something worth providing for your children. What's important now is to explore the best ways of *using* books so that you and your children get the most out of them.

The first thing to look at is how to fit books into family life. That's a question which involves several considerations. How often should you read to your children? When should you read to them? And how long should a reading session be?

It seems to me that you and your children are only going to get the full benefit from reading books together if you do it regularly. By regularly I mean something like once a day, every day, or at the very least, four or five times a week. Anything less than that and it's not really going to be a major part of family life at all. It may also be difficult for you to motivate yourself to read to your children unless you make it a *habit*. Life is busy enough for parents, and you'll find that there's always something else you could be doing.

You'll probably also discover that once you start reading to your children, once a day is about the least they'll let you get away with. Toddlers in particular can be especially persistent in their demands to be read to, and on some days you may find yourself being jabbed at knee level with a book every five minutes or so. Children who like books can have an almost insatiable appetite for them.

When you read to your children is up to you. As I've already said, I think it's a good idea to have a regular reading session at a particular time of day, and bedtime fits the bill nicely for all the reasons I've already outlined. It's a time for relaxed, gentle unwinding at the end of the day, when both you and your children are probably less under pressure. That's a very important consideration; the one thing a reading session needs to be is relaxed. Your child is not going to get very much out of a book, however good it is, if you're tearing through it because you've got to rush on to something else. As I'll explain a little further on, a book for children needs to be savoured, not gobbled up.

Nevertheless, that's no reason to restrict your reading sessions to one time a day. That's a minimum, and you'll find that your children will be delighted to have reading sessions at other times and in places other than at home. Reading a picture book to your three year old may take five minutes or less – and even the busiest parent should have a spare five minutes in the day! I've found myself reading books to my kids in the morning at breakfast, while they're in the bath, on rainy Sunday afternoons, in the middle of the night when they've woken up feeling sick or after a frightening nightmare. Think of books as a resource which you can always use to fill any spare moments with an activity of real interest and value.

If you're a two-partner household, remember that reading to the children is something you can and should share between you. Having two adults to read separately to children of different ages can solve a lot of problems and, as I've said, it's an activity in which fathers in particular can make a real contribution.

But it's also worth bearing in mind that other adults can always be press-ganged into reading service. Many a grandfather or grandmother, sister-in-law or single auntie's boyfriend can be persuaded to ease the burden on you by reading a few stories while they're around. Book-hungry children usually do the press-ganging themselves, if our house is anything to go by.

As far as the length of your reading sessions is concerned, the answer is always to take your cue from your kids. Babies and toddlers usually have quite short attention spans, so ten minutes may be more than enough at one time, although they may come back to you ten minutes later for another short session, and they can usually cope with lots of short books in a long session. As your child gets older, she'll be able to cope with longer sessions to match the longer books she'll enjoy, and you may find that by the age of five, half an hour is the minimum she'll put up with. By the age of eight she may want anything up to an hour for a bedtime story session.

That might sound a lot, but the thing that I've noticed over the years is that the more I've read to my children, the easier I've found it to fit those longer reading sessions in. Indeed, when you're reading a long story it might well be you who prolongs the reading session to find out what's going to happen, while your children doze off around you. I think that, in the end, how you fit reading to your children into your life depends on your attitude and your priorities. If you think it's worthwhile then you'll find a way to fit it into even the busiest schedule.

Your attitude towards children's books will be very positive if you enjoy using them with your children. I think that, if you give yourself a chance, that enjoyment will come naturally. Many of the books your children will enjoy at every stage will give you pleasure too, and you'll find that your children's delight in the books will rub off on you. It's a cumulative process. The more you enjoy the books together, the easier it will be for you and your children to give yourselves the excuse to have some fun with a reading session. Look on it as time off from the business of making a living and running a home – and we all need some time off occasionally.

You'll also need some time off occasionally from reading to your children. As you can imagine – and as you may already have discovered – it's nice to be wanted, but sometimes your children can want you (or want you to do something) a little *too* much. There will be times when you are too busy, or too tired, or ill, and when you simply don't want to read *Peter Rabbit* for the fifteenth time that day.

Many parents feel guilty if they say 'no' when a child asks them to read a story. But you shouldn't feel too guilty, especially if you do read books regularly to your children. It is all right to say no sometimes, if only to make sure that when you do read, it's at times when you really feel like it and want to. Just as there's no point in forcing a child to do something she doesn't enjoy, so there's no point in doing the same to yourself. It's important to keep the fun in your reading sessions – and that means that both you and your child should *want* to enjoy books together at a particular time.

It's also said sometimes that you should 'forget the housework', and read to your children instead. That's all very well, but the housework and a million and one other things have still got to be done some time. I remember that, when Thomas was born, I thought that I would let the housework slip for a few days and concentrate on making the girls feel involved and still loved, by reading them lots of stories, among other things. Eventually the nappy bucket was overflowing, none of us had any clean clothes to wear, there was nothing in the fridge, and every time I walked into the kitchen my feet stuck to the floor. So there will always be times when you *can't* read to your children, and you shouldn't feel guilty about that. Life must go on and, so long as reading is a part of family life, the occasional refusal doesn't matter too much.

This means, however, that from time to time books will be sources of argument between you and your child. Toddlers will throw tantrums when you say you don't want to read to them; older children will sulk and take out their anger on younger siblings, who will in turn find some way of inflicting their feelings on you. Nevertheless, such a refusal from a parent is all part of the process by which your child learns some important lessons; such as that everyone has their limits, and that you can't have what you want all of the time. Don't say no too often, though, which might lead to you getting out of the habit of reading to your children. Keep those regular story sessions going as much as you can. If you're like me, you'll probably find that story time is something you look forward to, anyway.

Reading stories

One thing you might be worried about is your ability to read stories aloud to your children in an interesting way. Reading aloud isn't something many of us have done since we were at school, and the very idea might fill you with dread. You might just feel rather embarrassed about reading aloud, a feeling which will not help you fire your children's interest in books and reading.

Some people also simply feel that reading a story about a rabbit that can talk, for example, is a little silly. The point to remember, however, is that your child doesn't think it's silly in that sense – she takes it very seriously. If you don't think of reading stories to your children as something which has worth in itself, then your children will hear your opinion of their stories and books in the very tone of your voice. That tone of voice will be telling them that you're not enjoying what you're doing, and will undercut the whole exercise.

I'm not saying that you should always read to your children in a hushed, serious tone of voice. What's important is that you should be prepared to put some effort into reading to your children. That will inevitably mean reading to your children in a style which is both appropriate to their age and to the type of book you're reading at any particular time.

If you do feel embarrassed or worried about reading to your children – don't. It's a very easy and pleasant activity, and your children are certainly not going to laugh at you. They'll do plenty of laughing *with* you as you both enjoy the books, and that sort of fun should chase away any embarrassment you might have. It will help if you look beforehand at the books you intend to read. Think of it as a rehearsal which will help to make sure there aren't any lines over which you stumble as you read the book to your children.

It should also help to build your confidence if you know what the story's about. You'll know whether the story's funny, whether it's got different characters in it, whether you need to make any special sounds – such as a lion roaring or a cow mooing – and so on. It's handy to know that these things will be expected of you!

In general terms, I've found that all children like a story to be read with *enthusiasm*. There's nothing that kills interest in a story so quickly as having it read in a dull, boring, droning monotone. Even the most exciting books can't survive treatment like that, and if your children are bored with a story, you will be, too.

The answer is to try and put some life into your reading. If there are several characters in a story, for example, do different accents for them. If there's a snake in the story, for example, give him a hissing, sibilant voice; make every 's' sound in what he says a hiss. It's a very simple thing, but it can add to the fun enormously. And don't think you can't do it – of course you can!

You'll probably find lots of ways of livening up stories in such a way if you go into it with that attitude in mind. Witches can have old, 'witchy' voices, lions can roar, cars can go 'toot! toot!' every time you see them. Sound effects of all sorts are always popular with children. In very simple terms, the more you put into reading stories, the more you and your children are going to get out of it.

Rhythm is important too, and it's worth reading a picture book text over to yourself to see if you can discover a hidden rhythm in it. There are quite a few books which are written in rhyme, such as _Peepo!_ – and whose rhythm is therefore obvious. Some of the best writers for children, though, produce texts which may not look rhythmic at first, but which reveal a real feeling of movement if you allow it to come through.

I'm thinking of a book such as _In the Night Kitchen_, by Maurice

Mickey's on his way in In The Night Kitchen _by Maurice Sendak
(Bodley Head and Puffin)._

Sendak. It's a strange-looking picture book about a child called Mickey, who falls out of bed and into a dream kitchen inhabited by three cooks who are all identical – they all look like Oliver Hardy of Laurel and Hardy! Now when I first used to read the story – which tells of how Mickey escapes being baked in a cake and gets the milk the cooks need – I thought it was very odd, not to say rather dull. But on subsequent readings I discovered that the words worked in a really rhythmic way, with lots of rhymes, and was soon reading it at a cracking pace, even singing bits of it. I love 'performing' *In the Night Kitchen*, and all my kids seem to enjoy it too. None of us are sure we understand the book – but who cares? It's lots of fun, and the secret was in letting the rhythm of the words come out naturally by itself.

In the same way it's an asset if you can develop some real theatrical skills, especially as you start to get into longer stories. The best stories for children feature the techniques which make any story worth hearing – a build up of tension, a climax, perhaps a surprise ending. It's worth looking at the stories you read your children to see if you can enhance these effects by pausing at moments of suspense, speeding up the reading during the exciting parts (such as a chase), or by giving it all you've got when the hero pops through the door at the end and shouts 'surprise!'

I can't stress enough the importance of reading to your children with as much verve and panache as you can. It makes all the difference to your children's enjoyment, and to yours. If you feel that you need some more tips on how to read stories, I can give you no better advice than to listen to and to watch how the professionals do it – that is, try to observe how professional actors and actresses read children's stories on television. You'll find that some are much better than others, and that the best are the ones who seem to be talking directly to a child with enthusiasm and enjoyment – and if you try to do the same, you won't go far wrong.

You may find that it's worth reading some picture books rather slowly so that you can spend some time looking at the pictures with your child. It might sound obvious, but adults often tend to focus on the *words* at the expense of the illustrations in a

Spot the visual jokes in Anthony Browne's Gorilla _(Julia MacRae and Magnet)._

children's book. You may have finished the one or two lines of text and have turned the page to get on with the story before your child has even had a chance to start looking at the pictures properly. Indeed, you'll probaby find that quite often you hardly see the pictures at all, and that your child picks out interesting details that you would have missed entirely.

It's worth bearing in mind that although words, stories and learning to read are all important, it's just as important to develop your child's _visual_ imagination. In fact it's probably the lack of emphasis in our education system on _looking_ at the world around us (and the emphasis on words and reading) that turns us into the sort of parents who don't stop to look at some of the amazing artwork in children's books today. That's why it's worth taking your time to look at the pictures in books by an artist such as Anthony Browne, for example, an illustrator who uses the techniques of surrealism to surprise and delight children. In his book _Gorilla_, for example, it's easy to rush on with the story and miss the delightful visual jokes dotted throughout which makes it worth stopping and looking at every page with care.

Taking the time to delight in such things can be extended to the story itself. If you've enjoyed a book, why not read it again – straightaway? Or if you've enjoyed a particularly clever, or funny part of a story, why not go over it again? You could talk about the book and how it works, why you like it, what you like about it. You could ask your children what they like about it and get them to talk about the story and the characters. It's in these ways that you'll help to maximise the value you get out of any particular reading session.

As far as longer books are concerned – that is, books for five- to eight-year-olds or even older – don't be put off by the length. A longer book can be read in sections over a period of time. We're reading Mary Norton's *The Borrowers* at the moment, at the rate of a chapter – sometimes half a chapter – a night. If a book is exciting or interesting, then it probably doesn't matter how long it is. Indeed, what we've discovered recently is that a long book has its own delights. It's something to look forward to, something you can pick up where you left off with a feeling of familiarity. The anticipation of waiting to see what happens is more than half the fun.

All that I've said in this section only applies to books which *are* exciting and interesting. I'm afraid that if a book is dull and boring, then sometimes there's nothing you can do to save it. If you and your children are not enjoying a book, then there's certainly no need to press on to the end; give it up and move on to something else which you find more enjoyable. The only problem here is that from time to time you and your children are going to disagree on what constitutes a dull and boring book – a subject which I'll be coming back to.

One final word on your reading style. I've always enjoyed doing 'funny voices' when reading stories, much to the annoyance of my daughter Helen. She likes a story to be read straight, without foreign accents or funny ways of talking. That's something I've just had to accept sometimes. Such a prohibition shouldn't stop you from reading with verve and enthusiasm, but I think it's a wish that should be respected, and you can bet that one of your children will at some time tell you to 'read it properly'. After all, they're the consumers, and as they used to say in shops – the customer is (almost) always right.

Reading to more than one child

Most parents soon find that they have to read to two or more children together, at least occasionally. It happens because, if you've got two children, a pre-schooler and a toddler, for example, you may well put them to bed at around the same time, which means they'll probably both want stories. Before we had our third child we used to read to the two girls separately, which is fine if you're a two-parent household. But if you're not, or if you're not both always around at story time, then the only solution is to read to the children together. And if you're mad enough to have three or more children – like us – you'll always be outnumbered anyway.

If the youngest of the children you're reading to is a baby or a toddler, and the oldest is a beginner reader, a seven- or eight-year-old, then you may have a few attention problems to face. The oldest child may well be a little bored by some of the baby books the youngest enjoys, and a baby or toddler is simply not going to be able to follow the story in the longer books your older child wants to hear. The answer in this case is to try and find something which will keep one child occupied while you read to the other. That could mean letting your baby or toddler look at books or play with toys while you read a chapter of a book to your seven-year-old; it could mean getting your older child to draw pictures while you read a board book to your baby.

I'm also a great believer in getting older children to participate in reading to the younger ones. In fact, you may find that quite often an older child is more than willing to do so, particularly if she's reading books that she enjoyed reading when she was younger herself. It's not something I'd force an older child to do – that simply wouldn't work – but it can be something you can persuade them to do. It can also help to improve an older child's developing reading skills.

It's probably easier to read to children together if they're in one of two groups. Babies and toddlers can often appreciate much the same books; there's a considerable overlap in their areas of interest. The same is true of pre-schoolers and the five to eights. I've found in the latter case that a four year old can actually keep up with and appreciate a quite complicated story if it's exciting or interesting enough. That in itself is a good thing; it seems to me that it's always worth trying to stretch your children's reading stamina and raise their sights from time to time, at any age.

Group reading sessions do have their problems, however, the main one being your children's behaviour. The image of two or three children clustered around a parent reading a favourite bedtime story, everyone intent on the book and the children perfectly behaved, is an appealing one. Unfortunately it's often not like that. Sometimes it is, but the reality is likely to involve two of the children arguing, pulling each other's hair, while the baby is desperately trying to get his teeth (literally) into the book, one of his sisters or anything within reach. Many is the time when I have brought a reading session to a sudden halt because of appalling behaviour on the part of my children. One common source of argument is, of course, who gets to choose the books, and a burst of sulking caused by a particular book *not* being the very next one to be read is so common as to be unremarkable. I'm often the one doing the sulking.

Frankly, there's not a lot you can do about all this. It's simply part of parenthood's rich tapestry, and the best I can do is counsel patience. It isn't always like that, however, and in general, if the stories are good and you read them in an interesting way, you should hold your children's attention most of the time. Occasionally during riotous bedtime reading sessions it will become apparent that tiredness (yours or your children's) is the main culprit. The answer then is to hasten bedtime and leave the stories for another day.

It is worth bearing in mind that each of your children will greatly appreciate being read to *alone* from time to time. It's only fair, after all, that your child should get some individual attention without having that pesky baby brother or snooty older sister butting in every five minutes. So if it's at all possible, do try to set aside some time regularly for reading alone to each child – even if it's only five or ten minutes every so often.

I've found that it pays to be strictly fair in group reading sessions with Emma and Helen. We have turn and turn about; first Helen chooses a book, which we read, then it's Emma's choice. I try to ensure that each child's total reading time is about the same, so if I've read one entire short book to Helen, Emma gets a complete chapter of her longer book which is, I hope, of roughly the same length. It seems to work most of the time.

Nevertheless, there are lots of occasions when one child will be bored by another child's choice – and when you will be, too. I've found that children can be very unadventurous in their choices. If you tell your pre-schooler to choose a book for a reading session, she'll probably choose the same one at least seven times out of ten. That's partly because it's her favourite, and also because it's easier to choose the one with which she's familiar, than to spend her time choosing one which might be a disappointment.

In this situation, a certain amount of compromise is necessary. You might well feel like saying 'Oh no, not that one again!', but it's important not to look down on her choice too obviously. After all, she has a right to her own opinions, and she may well not like the sort of books you do. Besides, her favourite books might really have something about them which strikes a chord with her, and it's usually worth looking at a child's favourite stories to see what's important to her, or what's bothering her at a particular time.

However, even though it's important to allow your child to develop her own ability to choose according to her tastes and preferences, there's plenty of reason occasionally to help her out and break the cycle of reading the same book over and over again. I've done that with all three of my children at different times, usually by offering to read a new book _as well as_ the old favourite at first.

Later you can replace the old favourite with new favourites. In that way you should keep reading sessions fresh and interesting – but never underestimate the ability of those old favourites to say something to your child for many years. So don't always try to

"Hello, monster," he said to the monster.

Bernard meets the monster in Not Now, Bernard *by David McKee (Andersen Press).*

force new books, or books *you* like, on to your child. That will probably only be counter-productive. Better to put up with a certain amount of boredom and wait for your child to show interest in something new herself later on, which she'll probably do anyway.

Ghosts, gremlins and nightmares

One reason for your child not liking a particular book is that she might find it frightening or disturbing in some way. This is quite common, and it's something to watch out for. It isn't always the most obvious stories that some children find upsetting, either. Your child might listen to tales of ghosts, and ghouls and monsters without batting an eyelid – only to have nightmares caused by a story about a child who gets harmlessly lost in the forest.

One book which my children refused point blank even to look at for a while was *Not Now, Bernard*, by David McKee. This classic picture book has a hero, Bernard, who discovers a monster in his garden. He tells his parents, but all they say is. . .'Not now, Bernard.' Then the monster eats Bernard and goes into the house. . .only to find that Bernard's parents ignore him in exactly the same way as they ignored the little boy who formed his meal.

Not Now, Bernard is deservedly popular with many children, and owes its appeal to the quality that frightened and disturbed my kids. Parents _do_ sometimes ignore their children when they shouldn't, and children are very much aware that they depend on their parents to take notice of them if they're to survive and be protected. What's disturbing in _Not Now, Bernard_ is that it's poor Bernard who suffers – he's the one who gets eaten up, although he's tried to save himself. My children have now grown to see the funny side of the story – but I think you can see why such a book might prove worrying to a small child.

That's why it's wise to be careful about the books you read to your children, and to be sensitive to their feelings about particular books. If your child finds something disturbing about a book, there's certainly no point in forcing it on her; such an action would only be cruel. There are plenty of other books, so you should be able to find something less upsetting. It's a good idea to look through the books you intend to read to your children with this sort of reaction in mind. Indeed, you know your children best, and you'll probably soon be able to look at a particular sort of book and decide whether it's potentially frightening for any of your children.

It is a difficult area, though, for often there's a very blurred boundary line between a book that speaks directly to some of your child's main concerns and a book that she will find frightening. I've already talked about the power of fairy tales to focus attention on some of the things that might concern your child in a very deep way. At times in your child's young life that power will be too disturbing; at others it will be just what she wants. Sensitivity in this context is very important on your part.

The power of a story to disturb is something I'm particularly aware of when it comes to reading sessions before bed. A tired child may be very much more open to suggestion, much more receptive to the power of a tale which could sink into her unconscious and brew trouble. I've got too much experience of children waking as a result of a nightmare brought on by something they've read or seen on the television not to know that it's a possibility. It's something that seems to affect pre-schoolers and five- to eight-year-olds in particular, and also those children with vivid imaginations.

This doesn't mean that you have to avoid books which can stimulate such a child; far from it. In one sense, occasional nightmares or 'bad thoughts', as my children call them, are part of the price you pay for opening your child's imagination to the rich variety of stories that she wants and needs to experience. One way of keeping this negative side of reading stories in perspective, and of limiting its bad effects, is to talk about the stories you read with your children *while you're reading them.* You can stop and say, 'This is a scary story, isn't it? Shall we stop? Is it too frightening for you?' Or you can say, 'That's scary, isn't it, to be caught by a wolf/bad witch/monster . . . do you think little Red Riding Hood/Hansel and Gretel/the hero will get away?'

Sometimes your children will want you to stop reading that story; sometimes they won't. After all, a lot of scary stories are popular *because* they scare you. We all like the thrill of being frightened sometimes, and children feel the same. . .otherwise why would a toddler enjoy being thrown into the air? The answer in that case is that your toddler knows she'll be caught safely – although the thrill is there because there's always an element of doubt. In the same way scary stories are good ways of exploring lots of frightening possibilities in the comfort of your own bedroom, with mum or dad sitting right next to you for protection.

Of course it's equally as important to talk about the non-scary books you read to your children. You'll find sometimes, especially with pre-schoolers, that your child will interrupt you with a stream of questions about all aspects of the book, its story, pictures and characters. Some of these questions will be un-answerable ('Why is the ball green?') but most deserve the fullest answer you can give. It's all part of enjoying a book, after all, and sometimes your child might not understand parts of a story, or words, or something in a picture. That can spoil her enjoyment – and can even worry her ('Where has Gretel gone? Has the witch eaten her?'). And if you're reading one of those special situation books – about illness, handicap or death, for example – then obviously it's very important to talk about the book and the subject as much as possible. That's what they're for, after all.

I also think it's perfectly legitimate sometimes to abbreviate or even to censor a story. For example, with _Not Now, Bernard_, my children decided that they wanted to look at it again so long as we missed out the page on which it said 'The monster ate Bernard'. After a while they decided to risk a reading of that page, too, and eventually we read the whole book through, with no adverse after effects.

I've often missed out frightening pictures, or skimmed over particularly graphic descriptions in some of the fairy tales we've read, by popular request. I always talk such 'censorship' over with the children, though. I don't want to impose my standards on them. We only miss out the things _they_ want to avoid and, wherever possible, we put them in as soon as we think we're all ready to cope.

It's also okay sometimes to abbreviate longer books for younger readers without such protective censorship in mind. I'm thinking of looking at information books, for example, with toddlers. Thomas has often enjoyed looking at interesting pictures in a book that's meant for a much older child. He doesn't need to have it read to him, but it helps if you can come up with an abbreviated 'commentary' to link the pictures in some way.

I have to confess that, from time to time, I also change the words in some picture books simply because they don't sound right – perhaps the author's missed the chance of a rhyme or an additional bit of rhythm. I've occasionally done that unconsciously while reading a book my children know and like, much to their disgust. You'll often find that children don't like to hear changes in familiar stories – even if daddy's version _is_ better!

Avoiding stereotypes

In recent years there's been a great deal of debate about sexism and racism in children's books. You should be aware that children's books are just as liable to be sexist and racist as any

Two bad babies,
with their breakfasts on their heads.

2

A scene from The Bad Babies' Counting Book *by Tony Bradman and Debbie van der Beek (Piccadilly Press).*

other form of book, and some books of the past that are still available do deal in stereotypes and have racist overtones. Publishers, authors, illustrators and many other people involved with children's books are increasingly aware of such issues, and it's encouraging to see that, in recent years, more and more books are being published which avoid stereotypes of a sexist kind (mother wearing an apron and standing at the sink, father reading the paper while he waits for his breakfast). There's also been a heartening increase in the number of books which reflect the multi-cultural nature of our society in a positive way, and the fact that more and more children are growing up in one parent families.

There's still a long way to go, however; something that was brought most forcefully to my attention as far as the multi-cultural issue was concerned by children's television presenter Floella Benjamin when we were judging the first *Parents* Best Books for Babies Award. As Floella pointed out, children become very attached to favourite books; their books are a very important part of their lives. It's therefore vital that a black child should have plenty of books which reflect the reality of his or her life – that is, books with children like him or her in them. Then it can be – in Floella's words – 'my book'. It's a point I hope publishers will continue to bear in mind when it comes to producing books for children – we need books which *all* our children can enjoy and feel that way about.

Dealing with TV

I've already said that I don't think television is as bad as some people might have you believe. Indeed, there are some programmes which I would positively encourage parents to allow their children to watch. These are programmes which help your child to learn in an entertaining way. *Sesame Street* is just such a programme; its lots of fun, *and* educational.

I would go further and say that I see no reason to stop your children from watching non-educational programmes on television – why shouldn't they just enjoy themselves sometimes? However, I will admit that television can be a problem – occasionally a major one. There are three main areas which it's worth looking at; the amount of television your child (and the family as a whole) watches; the sorts of programmes she's exposed to; and what television (especially unrestricted television of the wrong sort) can do to your child's mind.

Many families these days put the television on as soon as they get up in the morning, leave it on all day, and turn it off only when they stagger up to bed, eyes red and smarting from hour after hour of flickering images. From time to time newspapers print statistics that show very high numbers of quite young children to be up late at night watching television, and it's probable that many of today's children watch hours of television every day. This isn't a very good state of affairs. As others before me have said (most notably Jim Trelease), a child who is watching television *isn't* doing something else; she isn't playing in the garden, she isn't painting a picture, she isn't talking to her father, she isn't running, or climbing, or reading a book. Instead she's sitting in front of a little box that gives her a very low level of stimulation.

It's very easy to slip into a way of life in which television becomes the centre of everything. It can kill conversation between parent and child, it can stop you thinking, and it can keep you pinned in your armchair when you'd probably enjoy doing something else much more.

Something else comes out of the statistics, and that's the unpleasant fact that many young children must be watching programmes which are unsuitable for them. In general, television stations tend to screen programmes with a high level of violence or sex later on in the evening, with the express purpose of making sure that children don't see them. Unfortunately it's obvious that many children do see such programmes, and I for one don't like the idea that seven and eight year olds (and sometimes even younger children) are being exposed to programmes which even I find frightening or unpleasant.

The problem has been made worse by the rise of the video. A late-night 'adult' film can be taped and then watched in the afternoon. It's also been possible for quite some time for you to hire or buy a real video nasty and watch it in your own home. Recent reports have indicated that many young children are being shown such videos – and I think that the idea of a seven-year-old watching a film like *The Texas Chainsaw Massacre* is not only depressing and worrying, but frightening, too.

That sort of film is an obvious and extreme example of the way in which television can be misused. But television can present problems of a more subtle, more insidious kind. I'm talking about the propaganda that slips out of your television set about the way of life you should lead, the sort of things that you should buy, the sort of people you should be. It's important to remember that television is an enormously powerful medium which is used by all sorts of different people and groups of people to put across the messages they want you to swallow. Sometimes those messages are inoffensive or even beneficial. . .a lot of the time they're manipulative and very dangerous.

Advertising is a major culprit in this area. I have no objections to it in principle, but I do object to the way it's sometimes used to manipulate children's desires. However good the children's programmes might be, they're often ruined by the commercials which break them up and stimulate in your children a desire for all sorts of products. Many young children aren't all that sure of the difference between a commercial and a programme anyway, and the line has been increasingly blurred in recent years in any case.

Manufacturers and TV companies have now realized that very big profits can be made out of young children – and that means out of you – through television. The idea is simple; all you do is come up with a character, or set of characters, and develop them simultaneously as a product and a television series. The television exposure stimulates sales of the toys, and all the other spin-offs, from stationery to books, and you can further stimulate activity at the cash till with advertising.

I'm not saying that the products aren't worth what you pay for them, or that they don't give your children pleasure. But you should remember that what appears on the screen in your home is often the result of some very hard-nosed calculations about how to separate you from your money by means of making your children want things they've never even heard of before. Even if you're aware of all that, and you don't succumb to the pressure, it's worth bearing in mind that television is _never_ neutral. All those programmes come complete with a set of assumptions about the way we should run our lives, assumptions that your children can soak up before you're even aware of them.

Those assumptions can be many and varied. For example, your child might watch a cartoon in which the female characters do all the cooking and look after the men characters, who are big, rough and tough and order everyone about. It might seem unimport- ant. . .after all, it's only a cartoon. But you should multiply that one cartoon by all the hours your child spends in front of the television in her young childhood, and then you might have some idea of how powerful a medium television can be in supporting stereotypes of that sort.

Programme makers have been made to become increasingly aware in recent years of this problem, and many programmes now go out of their way to be non-sexist and non-racist. Some programmes for children are even designed to tackle these issues head on and promote more equality and more thought about the ways in which we run our lives and society. But many are unreformed in their sexism and racism, perhaps unconsciously, sometimes. If you want a better society in the future, one in which people aren't discriminated against on the grounds of their sex, colour or religion, then it's worth being aware of the sort of assumptions which lie behind much of the television your child is watching – even those harmless-seeming cartoons.

The last point to be made about television is that, in general, watching it is a very passive occupation. It does everything for you; once you've turned on the set, all you have to do is sit back and let it wash over you. I once heard Shirley Hughes, one of our leading author/illustrators for children, discussing just this issue on the radio. As she said, television provides you with pictures. . .unlike a book which helps you to make pictures in your head. Because those moving pictures are so real, they tend not to stimulate any sort of interpretation or deeper thought. Books do just that. . .your mind has to work at least a little to make the connections, call characters into being in your mind, interpret and see beyond what's there on the page. As Shirley Hughes says, picture books with stories can help children to do that, they're *stimulating*. Used properly, an interesting book can really help a young mind to start working and developing. Television can close the doors that books can open.

Television used properly, however, *can* open doors – even doors that lead to books. So how do you control the beast? The simple answer is to turn it off. That's harder than it sounds, but it's got to be done, at least from time to time. I believe very strongly that children should only be allowed to watch programmes that are appropriate for them, and that you should help them learn to be discriminating about what they watch. If you notice that your child is bored by a programme – as children often are – don't let her switch over, suggest that she switch the television off and that she do something else. It's worth planning your viewing ahead, in fact, by finding out what programmes are coming up and choosing to watch the ones that are interesting. It's important to help your child learn that television is a tool which can be used, but which needs to be controlled and kept in perspective.

It's also important for you to try and watch television _with_ your child as far as possible. Often there are things about programmes which need to be explained, especially to very young children. Your toddler may not understand, for example, that an elephant is larger than a mouse if both appear on the screen the same size.

It's also important to remember that your child might be disturbed or upset by something that seems perfectly innocent, in the same way as she might be upset by a book. Your child might start off watching her favourite programme, and then find herself watching a Tom and Jerry cartoon which is full of frantic action and violence. In cartoons of that type everything turns out all right in the end, but some children simply can't take the tension. Helen is one of those children who often ends up hiding behind the sofa instead of watching such a programme. I was one myself.

One way of weaning a child off television and on to books is to give her a book that's related to a programme. There's an increasing amount of cross-fertilisation between children's television and children's books, with good books being turned into programmes, and programmes leading to spin-off books. Programmes for younger children often feature stories from books, too. This isn't always simply another marketing hype. If your child enjoys a particular story on television or a particular programme, then that's your cue to set off for the bookshop or library to get hold of the book in question.

You could also do it the other way round, by getting videos of classic books such as _The Wind in the Willows_, or that all-time classic and favourite with all young children, _Mary Poppins_. It's also worth looking into the possibility of getting story tapes for your child, many of which come with books. Apart from being ideal for things like car journeys, story tapes can add a new dimension to your child's interests. Your local public library may well have both videos and tapes for hire at a very small fee.

More about reading

I've already looked briefly at the subject of learning to read, but it's a subject which assumes very great importance for most parents, so it's worth a more in-depth look. What I've always been particularly interested in, at any rate, is how I can help my children learn to read – and there's lots to be said about that.

When your child goes to school, she'll probably work through a reading scheme. The books in a reading scheme are very carefully graded. That means they're designed to introduce your child to new words or types of words in a gradual way. Often they sound very strange when you read them. . .one that Helen brought home had a story about Bill (not Jack) and Jill on a hill, and it was very flat and monotonous in comparison to many books which weren't designed as part of a reading scheme.

In the past, too – and it may still happen to some parents in certain areas – parents were encouraged *not* to get involved in the process by which their children learned to read. The attitude in many schools was that reading should be left to 'the professionals', and that the best thing parents could do was not to 'interfere', although it was recognized that for parents to at least be interested in what their children were doing could be of great help.

Times have changed, mostly as a result of a debate in educational circles which has centred on the way in which children learn to read. Because of a continuing change in attitudes, too, parents are increasingly being seen as the greatest hidden resource available to schools in helping children learn to read.

I suppose the best way of describing this change in attitudes is to say that it's a move away from the idea of *teaching* children to read towards that of helping them *learn*. Increasingly, specialists working in this field are talking about the *continuity* of the way children learn.

Remember, when your child was born she couldn't talk at all; she had absolutely no grasp of language whatsoever. But by the time she starts school she's probably a fluent – even excessive, if my children are anything to go by – talker. You certainly didn't sit down and *teach* her to talk. She more or less picked it up as she went along, with your help, of course. Your child learns to talk by talking and being talked to, and what you do is to correct her, encourage her and provide her with the raw material she needs – that is, plenty of conversation.

There's a whole school of thought which says that children can learn to read in the same way. Their theory is that, just as you learn to ride a bike by actually riding it, children learn to read by being readers. That means they need real stories, real reading experiences which focus on their interests and needs and stretch them rather than limit them. This school of thought maintains that the flat, monotonous, artificial structure of reading scheme books limits children and – more importantly – takes all the interest out of reading. Supporters of the 'learning to read through reading' school say that it would be possible to dispense entirely with reading schemes and help children learn to read by exposing them to plenty of interesting and exciting children's books.

In my own experience I've found that children are keen to learn to read if they see that books are enjoyable. If there's a point to learning to read, then a child will be enthusiastic, and many children who have had experience of lots of good children's books before school do learn to read virtually without help. In that sense I'm in full agreement with the anti-reading-scheme groups – children do learn to read through reading, by making mistakes and having them corrected, by being interested. But what exactly does that mean? And where does it leave you, the parent?

What it means is that your child needs to be encouraged to take part in the experience of reading a book from a very early age. She needs to be encouraged to look at the pictures, point to the things that are mentioned, and helped to understand that the printed words on the page represent the words that come from your mouth as you read it. It means encouraging your child to retell stories that she's learned by heart, and talking about the characters in her books.

I've often seen Thomas lying in bed 'reading' a book to himself. Even though he still can't say very much, he goes through familiar books, turning pages, looking at the pictures, 'telling' himself the story, and usually ends up falling asleep with a book over his face. As he gets older, he will, like Helen and Emma, begin to learn books off by heart, and gradually, words will become familiar on the page until, one day, he'll be reading. He'll need plenty of help on the way, but it's important to stress that it's all part of a continuous process that can begin early in babyhood.

I stress the word 'continuous', because your involvement shouldn't stop when your child starts school. It's almost certain that she'll have an involvement of some sort with a reading scheme, and as I said earlier, I think that such schemes, when used in a flexible way, do have real benefits; children often enjoy them, however boring they might sound to you or I. But it's still vital for you to continue to read interesting and exciting books to your beginner reader – and also to listen to her read as often as possible.

Most teachers these days will more than welcome your positive involvement and support. Remember, you're just as important as the teachers in any case. It's the preparation you give your child before she starts school and the help and support you give her once she's started that can make all the difference.

One very practical and active way for you to become involved in your child's school, which will at the same time help in her reading – and help her schoolmates, too – is to set up and run a **school bookshop**. There are thousands of such bookshops in existence, and they range from small cupboards which contain only a limited range of books, to quite large affairs with a wide variety of stock. Many of them are run by enthusiastic teachers – but parents get involved too, and they're often the driving force.

It isn't as complicated as you might think, and the whole idea behind setting up a school bookshop is very simple. If it's hard to take children to where the books are, then why not take the books to the children? A school bookshop can be a most valuable resource in a school and help to make a contribution in almost every area. Most important, it can make buying books an easy and normal part of your child's life. There are also some school book clubs which can operate independently or in conjunction with the school bookshop.

The work of most school bookshops is co-ordinated by The School Bookshop Association, which also produces an excellent magazine called *Books for Keeps* (details on page 116).

It can sometimes happen, however, that a child who's just started school seems to go off books and being read to at home for a while. It happened with Emma when she started school. She had been more than happy to read to for hours on end, but suddenly she wasn't interested at all. She wanted to spend bedtime copying letters and drawing, and she was adamant that she didn't want to be read to. It was a worry for a while, but in the end we worked out that it was something of an energy problem. Poor Emma was putting so much into her day at school and learning to read that she didn't have any energy left over at the end of the day to immerse herself in stories. She wanted to give her brain a rest, which was fair enough.

So for a few months we gave her books a holiday, although I continued to offer to read to her. Then gradually, as she began to find it easier to cope with the demands her school day made on her, she became interested in books again. I tried not to force it, although I did get a bit grumpy about not being able to read to her once or twice. Finally I suggested that we read _Fairy Tales_ by Terry Jones and, although she was reluctant at first, she agreed. . .and since then there's been no stopping her. If your child reacts in the same way when she starts school, the secret is, I think, not to put pressure on her or let her feel that you thinks books and reading is fantastically important.

In my experience, that's a sure-fire way of putting your child right off. It's better to let it go for a while, and then to try and come up with a book that she'll find irresistible – that could be anything, from a book like _Fairy Tales_ to a joke book. But don't panic – so long as there are books around and available in your home, and you make the offer, your child will come back to them in the end, especially if she's enjoyed them before.

You sometimes come across children – even quite young children – who, according to their parents, have never been interested in books at all. How do you turn a child like that into a reader? It's not a problem I've ever had to face with any of our children – it's usually a question of which book to read next, rather than wondering whether we should be looking at books at all. However, I suspect that many children who aren't interested in reading have never been read an interesting book. I've never met a child who isn't entranced by a book like _Where's Spot?_ or

Where the Wild Things Are. And once a child has had experience of one or two books like that, she'll want more; whether she gets any more is up to you.

In the same way, there are many, many books around which might get an older child interested in reading. Obviously it's a question of finding the right one, and there's only one way of doing that – trial and error. You do have the advantage of knowing your child, of knowing her likes and dislikes and interests. So it might be that a book with a ballet theme, or a book about horses or cars might just do the trick. So long as *you're* interested enough to keep trying, you should manage eventually to come up with something which will interest your child. Once you've done that, it's a question of building on the basis you've established.

One final point on this subject – I'm certainly in favour of encouraging your child to read anything to get her interested. If that means comics, or 'annuals', or cheap spin-offs from television programmes, that's fine. It might just make her interested enough in reading to progress – with your help – to something that's a bit better. But many comics are quite harmless in themselves – and besides, when I was a kid I always had my nose stuck in a Superman comic (when it wasn't in a book or pointing at the television!). Tape cassettes – many of which come with a book – can also be a help in getting a child interested in reading.

4
Choosing and buying books

Children's books, you may agree by now, are wonderful things. But where do you get them? And how can you afford to pay for them? The first question might sound daft – but it isn't. There are many bookshops in which you'll find children's books, and there are, of course, plenty of libraries where they can be found too. But the fact of the matter is that there aren't enough of either, and you may find yourself in one of the many areas where your nearest supply of children's books is quite some distance away.

We parents have an added problem in that it's often difficult for us to get about when the children are along. Setting out on a shopping trip with two or three small children is bad enough if you've got a car, but it can be very tough indeed if you have to rely on buses or trains. Getting round the shops is also hard for parents, especially if you've got a pushchair or pram. Shops and shopping centres are not designed for young families, as anyone will tell you who's been faced with the prospect of getting up two flights of stairs to the children's clothes department with a pushchair, a baby and a demanding toddler in tow.

All of which can make it very difficult to provide your children with the books they want and need. The other problem, the cost of the books, is also one which every parent will understand. If there's one thing that most young families have in common, it's a lack of money. Budgets are usually very tight when the children are small, and you probably feel that you have to have a very good reason for spending money on something that might not seem like an essential, in the way that food or clothes are. It's true, too, that books can be very expensive – and the price of books is going up all the time, just like most other things.

In this section I hope to tell you how you can get round both problems. There are plenty of libraries and bookshops around, but there are also ways of getting the books to come to you rather than going to find the books. Providing your child with wonderful books needn't bankrupt you, either.

It's worth pausing to give the subject of value for money some thought, in any case. I think that books can represent terrific value for money. There aren't many products that you can use over and over again and, if you provide your child with the right books, that's exactly what will happen. I can think of a number of picture books we've got that we've read now to three different children time and time again. Each picture book may cost quite a lot to buy, but if you divide the original cost by the *hundreds* of times you read the book, then it's obvious that you're getting a lot of entertainment for a little money. And the cheaper the book, the more value for money you're getting.

If you think about it in those terms, a book represents much better value than many toys. It also represents much better value than a bar of chocolate or a fizzy drink – and it's better for your child's health and teeth! In fact, for the cost of half a dozen bars of chocolate you could probably buy your toddler a paperback picture book which might give her pleasure for months, and then can be handed on to a brother or sister – or even your toddler's children, years later!

That is, of course, provided your toddler doesn't draw on it, chew it or otherwise generally do it damage. I have to admit that children do sometimes do unspeakable things to their books, and there's nothing more frustrating for a parent than to find an expensive new book defaced within a day or two of it having been bought. But children do the same thing to toys, and my daughters seem capable, now they're at school, of getting through a pair of shoes in about a week and a half.

A certain amount of wear and tear on all your children's things is unavoidable, and toddlers seem to be the worst culprits. Thomas has recently had a spell of ripping pop-up books to pieces, and tends to look at me uncomprehendingly when I remonstrate with him about this habit. I shouldn't complain, really; I once spent a pleasant afternoon as a small child defacing the Bible – I think I've been paying for that particular sin ever since I became a parent.

It is possible, however, to make your children aware that it's wrong to deface or destroy books. A certain amount of damage is inevitable among books for babies and toddlers; most of our board books have the odd tooth mark or food stain. But I've found that if a child is interested in a book, she's unlikely to do it too much damage; children very soon realize that if a book is destroyed or defaced too badly, they won't get the experience they want out of it.

Of course, toddlers and even older children can be a little clumsy sometimes, and that can result in the odd torn page. A tantrum might lead to a few rips, too. What's surprised me most however about the way my children treat their books is the respect they show for them – and that's a respect based on interest. Even Thomas is usually very careful, especially with his favourites. It is possible to repair books, too, with a little sticky tape and a bit of effort.

Obviously, though, you'll want to make sure that the books you give your children are sturdy and well produced in any case. It's worth looking at any books you're thinking of buying for your child with possible destruction in mind, especially where babies and toddlers are concerned. Small board books, for example, are sometimes liable to splitting down the spine, something it's worth looking at carefully before you buy. Pop-up and novelty books too are often a little fragile, and you may even come across a pop-up which hasn't been produced properly. I've come across books in which the mechanisms don't work at all – so it's always worth checking them before you pay out your money. Equally, it's worth giving any book a quick examination to make sure that it's got all its pages and that they're in the right order. Booksellers will exchange a genuinely faulty book, but it's very frustrating to get home and find that the climax of the story is missing!

Using your library

All my kids belong to the library, and it's well worth getting your child joined up as soon as you can – perhaps even at birth! It doesn't cost anything, and most libraries have a children's section. That children's section is more than likely to contain books for all ages – from babies upwards. Many children's libraries are very welcoming, friendly places, too, with little chairs and tables for the kids, cosy corners where they can sit and read through the books before choosing which ones to take home.

A family outing to the library can be lots of fun, and it's something that's worth taking your time over. You'll probably find that your children will need a certain amount of help in finding the books that are right for them. That might mean that you'll need some help, too, and if there's one person it's worth cultivating, it's your friendly local children's librarian. They're the experts, and you'll find that they really do know about children's books, especially the books in their own library! If you want to know what books are right for your child, ask your librarian.

Libraries these days are also much more than places to find books, although that's still their main purpose. You're likely to find in your local library a range of story-tapes, records (including records for children) and video tapes (again, including films for children). Libraries are also often places where things happen, especially during the school holidays.

Our local libraries often have storytelling sessions for children in the holidays, so it's worth keeping your eye on the library notice boards – or finding out from the staff what's coming up. Libraries are also excellent sources of information about your area in general, and you'll find that they'll often have details of other book events, such as authors visiting local shops or special promotions like Children's Book Week.

As you can see, libraries are very different these days. If you remember them as forbidding places where a rule of total silence was imposed and children were supposed only to be seen behaving well and certainly never, ever heard, then you're in for a pleasant surprise. Don't think that your tearaway toddler is going to get you chucked out of the library. . .so long as she doesn't cause absolute mayhem, she'll probably get away with a fair amount of noise.

You may sometimes come across a librarian who doesn't like children to make too much noise, but most children's librarians are happy to see children enjoying books. Nevertheless, one of the lessons I try to teach my kids about the library is that it's a place where they should show respect for others by not being too disruptive. And they've been taught that defacing, tearing or otherwise mangling a library book is a major crime!

And remember, while your kids are in the children's section of the library finding all sorts of wonderful books, why don't you have a look round the adult shelves? You never know, you might well find something there to interest you!

Buying books

There are other ways of getting hold of books for your children, ways which won't break the bank. Jumble sales are often a good source of children's books, especially school jumble sales. My daughters' school in fact always has a stall at its jumble sales on which you'll find toys and books together, and we've picked up several favourite books for a few pennies. Second hand and charity shops also often have children's books in their book section, and some libraries sell off old books very cheaply. Just because someone else doesn't want a book, it doesn't mean that it's no good – and you'd be surprised at how well looked-after many of these secondhand children's books are. And there are such things as secondhand bookshops.

I think that this is also an area where you could take some direct action, perhaps with your friends. You might go to a local mother and toddlers' group, or your children might go to a playgroup. Why not suggest that such a local group should have a regular book sale? As you'll discover, your children will outgrow many books, or there will be books that they don't like, and it's good to have an opportunity occasionally to clear the shelves and make room for some new reading matter.

Such an event could be held for charity, the idea being that parents donate old books to the group, and that all money raised goes to a nominated charity or to the group itself. I've found in exercises of this sort that you can raise quite a bit of money, and of course it's the kids who benefit in the end by getting some new books – which won't cost you very much. On a much smaller scale, it's also worth simply swapping books with your friends from time to time.

Of course all these books have to come from somewhere in the first place, and most of them are bought in a bookshop. Despite what I've said about libraries and secondhand books, I still think that it's important for your children to have some of their own brand new books if it's at all possible. Children love to have their own things, and you'll find that they can become very proprietorial about their books in particular.

One problem we've had to face is trying to explain to a young child the difference between 'borrowing' a book from the library which you have to return, and 'buying' a book from a bookshop, which you're allowed to keep forever. It's quite an important lesson, which sinks in eventually – so long as you go to both bookshops and libraries often enough!

From what I said at the beginning of this section about there not being enough bookshops in some areas, you'll realize that your first task is to find your bookshop. To make that easier I've included further on a list of bookshops broken down into areas, so you should be able to find one that's near (or relatively near, at least) where you live.

These are shops which sell children's books, and many of them specialise in books for the young. You should also bear in mind that most branches of W.H. Smiths and John Menzies sell children's books as well. Other large retail chains have in recent years begun to sell children's books; you may even find some in your local supermarket or newsagents.

You will in any case always be able to find *Ladybird* books in all sorts of outlets. These inexpensive, well produced little books are certainly worth getting hold of for your children. Like most post-war children, I grew up on them, and I've bought many for my children. They're usually excellent value for money, and they've been keeping up with the times as far as children's books are concerned.

I wouldn't like my children to exist solely on a diet of *Ladybird* books, though; they need other types of book, too. That's why you shouldn't be daunted by the reputation bookshops seem to have acquired over the years. As with libraries, many people think of a bookshop as a forbidding sort of place where you need to be quiet, and where you're virtually showing your ignorance simply by going in and not knowing what your're looking for. It seems that, where books are concerned, we tend to think of the places where they're to be found as somewhere different and not for ordinary mortals.

A bookshop, however, is simply a place where you can buy books, and you'll probably find that many of the specialist children's bookshops in particular are very welcoming places. Like up-to-date libraries, the best children's bookshops – and there are plenty of them around – may well have little chairs and tables, a selection of toys to play with, and staff who know lots about children's books. In fact, if you can find such a bookshop and cultivate your friendly local children's bookseller, you'll be doing your children a big favour – and saving yourself a lot of time and effort. A good bookseller who knows his or her stock and is interested in children's books can help you match the right book and child very quickly.

I'm also a great believer in allowing children as much leeway as possible in choosing their own books. You might think that your toddler won't have much idea about what books are best for her, but you'd be surprised at just how good children can become at working out which books are within their age range. Both in libraries as well as in bookshops, I tend to try and direct my children towards the areas where they'll find books which are roughly for their age range, and then allow them to do most of the choosing.

I often draw books to their attention though, especially if I come across one that I think one of my children will particularly like. And we have sometimes had quite lengthy discussions about whether a particular book is unsuitable or not. I try to go along with their choices as much as possible, and explain if I think a book is too long, or too difficult or too expensive. Sometimes I give in, usually to find that my children are right and that they do enjoy the book they've chosen. It's a 'to and fro' process, with guidance coming from you. With the right help you can help your children to develop their own tastes and independence in reading, and that's very important. It's also a good way for you to learn about what your child likes, too!

Don't worry too much about your children causing havoc and getting their grubby fingers on those nice, clean white pages. Good booksellers know that they have to show their stock in order to sell it, and therefore have sample copies of things like expensive pop-ups so that you can see how they work. Obviously, no bookseller is going to be too happy if your child starts chewing her way through the stock, but you shouldn't let the possibility that your child might misbehave in a bookshop stop you from entering one in the first place. In any case, I've found in general that children are usually too interested in the books to create much trouble – although there are always exceptions.

Like libraries, some bookshops are also good centres for information about your local area and any book events that might be taking place. Sometimes authors and illustrators visit shops to sign books, draw pictures and talk to the children. An event like that can be very exciting for your child. It's marvellous to see a child meeting the person who wrote or drew her favourite book, and if she walks away with a signed copy or a little picture dedicated to her, she might well become a life-long reader. There are plenty of such events, especially at certain times of the year. It's worth keeping an eye out for such things and going along – apart from anything else they're often a great day out.

Some bookshops reach out to the local community, too. There are booksellers who take books to schools in buses or vans, and booksellers who supply school bookshops. Some bookshops are involved in mail order and run book clubs, and all bookshops will gladly order books for you. Think of going into your local bookshop as a first step into a world of books; it's all there, and all you have to do for your children is to help them reach out and take it.

Bookshops

The following list is based on one published in _The Good Book Guide to Children's Books_, and is reproduced here in a revised form with permission.

The following shops stock children's books. Apologies to any that are missed out; omissions, it is hoped, will be corrected in future editions.

The Bookseller's Association can also supply you with the name of your nearest member of its Children's Group. Telephone: 01-739 8214.

London

Angel Bookshop, 102 Islington High Street, N1
Apollo Bookshop, 66 Avenue Road, Bexleyheath
Army & Navy Stores, Victoria Street, SW1
At the Sign of the Dragon, 131 Sheen Lane, East Sheen, SW14
Belsize Bookshop, 193 Haverstock Hill, NW3
Bookboat Co Ltd, Cutty Sark Gdns, Greenwich, SE10
Books Etc Ltd, 120 Charing Cross Road, WC2
Books Etc Ltd, 174 Fleet Street, EC4
Books Etc Ltd, 66/77 Victoria Street, SW1
Bookspread, 58 Tooting Bec Road, SW17
Bull & Sons, Brooksby House, Brooksby St, N1
Bush Books, 144 Shepherds Bush Centre, W12
Canonbury Bookshop, 268 Upper St, Islington, N1
Centerprise Bookshop, 136–138 Kingsland High Street, E8
Children's Bookshop, 29 Fortis Green Road, N10
Children's Bookshop, 66 High Street, Wimbledon, SW19
Children's World, 229 Kensington High St, W8
The Church House Bookshop, Great Smith Street, SW1
City Booksellers, 80 Cheapside, EC2
Collets Penguin Bookshop, 52 Charing Cross Road, WC2
Crouch End Bookshop, 60 Crouch End Hill, N8
Dillons University Bookshop, Malet Street, WC1
Ealing Books, 5 Central Buildings, Ealing Broadway, W5

Elgin Books, 6 Elgin Crescent, W11
Ellingtons (London) Ltd, 26 Market Place, NW11
Faculty Books, 98 Ballards Lane, N3
Fagins, 62 Chase Side, Southgate, N14
Fanfare Bookcentre, 2 Chingford Road, Walthamstow, E17
E. & W. Fielder, 54 Hill Road, Wimbledon, SW19
W. & G. Foyle Ltd, Charing Cross Road, WC2
Foyles Educational Ltd, 37 Upper Berkeley St, W1
Claude Gill Books, 19/23 Oxford Street, W1
  (also at James St & Piccadilly)
The Good Book Guide Bookshop, 91 Great Russell Street, WC1
Greenwich Book Company, 119 King George Street, SE10
Grenwich Book Company, 37 Neal Street, WC2
Harrods, Dept 681, Knightsbridge, SW1
Hatchards, 187 Piccadilly, W1
Roy Hayes, Chequers Parade, Passey Place, SE9
Heywood Hill, 10 Curzon Street, W1
High Hill Bookshop, 6-7 Hampstead High Street, NW3
Images, 16, Cecil Court, Charing Cross Rd, WC2
Islington Books, 268 Upper Street, Islington, N1
The Kilburn Bookshop, 8 Kilburn Bridge, NW6
Kings Bookshop, 17 Rugby Street, WC1
A. R. Mowbray, 28 Margaret Street, W1
Owl Bookshop, 211 Kentish Town Road, NW5
Passage Bookshop, 5 Canning Cross, SE5
Penguin Bookshop, Liberty & Co, Regent Street, W1
Puffin Bookshop, 1 The Piazza, Covent Garden, WC2
Reading Matters, Lymington Avenue, Wood Green, N22
Regent Bookshop, 73 Parkway, NW1
John Sandoe, 10 Blacklands Terrace, SW3
Selfridges, Dept 388, 400 Oxford Street, W1
Swiss Cottage Books, 4 Canfield Gdns, NW6
The Tinderbox, 26 Chase Side, Southgate, N14
T.H.A.P. Bookshop, 178 Whitechapel Road, E1
Waterstone's, 121-125 Charing Cross Road, WC2
Waterstone's, 99 Old Brompton Road, SW7
Writer's Cramp, 17 Flask Walk, NW3

Avon

Chapter & Verse, 86 Park Street, Bristol
Clifton Bookshop, 84 Whiteladies Road, Bristol 8
Durdham Down Bookshop, 39 North View,
Westbury Park, Bristol
Georges, 89 Park Street, Bristol
Grimly's Books, 16 High Street, Chipping Sodbury, Bristol
Milton's, 3,5,9 New Station Road, Fishponds, Bristol
The Nailsea Bookshop, 75 High Street, Nailsea, Bristol
Ogborns, 1 & 3 Bath Hill, Keynsham, Bristol
Pied Piper Bookshop, 65 Park Street, Bristol
Tridias, 8 Saville Row, Bath
Where the Wild Things Are, 26 Ambra Vale, Hotwells, Bristol
Whiteman's Bookshop, 7 Orange Grove, Bath

Bedfordshire

The Book Castle, 12 Church Street, Dunstable
Luton Bookshop, 42/44 Wellington Street, Luton
Pemberton Bookseller, 18 Mill Street, Bedford
Taylors Bookshop, 42 New Bedford Road, Luton

Berkshire

Carter & Wheeler, 272A High Street, Slough
Caversham Bookshop, 35 Prospect Street, Caversham, Reading
Everett's Bookshop, 17 Market Street, Maidenhead
Hammicks Bookshop, 1 King Edward Court,
Peascod Street, Windsor
Hungerford Bookshop, Kennett House, Hungerford
The London Street Bookshop, 35–39 London Street, Reading
Pan Bookshop, 123 Butts Centre, Reading
Town Bookseller, 1 Northbrook Street, Newbury
Town Bookseller, 4 Union Street, Reading

Buckinghamshire

The Chapter House, 12 Gregories Road, Beaconsfield
Chapter One, 15 Market Square, Chesham
Fagins Bookshop, 160 Midsummer Arcade, Secklow Gate East,
Milton Keynes

The Marlow Bookshelf, 36 West Street, Marlow
Weatherhead's Bookshop Ltd, 58 Kingsbury, Aylesbury

Cambridgeshire
The Bookshop, Godmanchester, Huntingdon
Heffers Children's Bookshop, 30 Trinity Street, Cambridge
St. Ives Bookshop, 12 The Broadway, St. Ives, Huntingdon
Websters Bookshops Ltd, 6 Queensgate Centre, Peterborough

Cheshire
Books Bradshaw, Nile Street, Warrington
"The Legend", 55 London Road, Alderley Edge
The Wise Owl, 6 High Street, Nantwich

Cleveland
Alan Douglas, 23 Church Square, Hartlepool
The Great Ayton Bookshop, 47 High Street, Great Ayton
The Guisborough Bookshop, 4 Chaloner Street, Guisborough
Thorne's Student Bookshop Ltd, 165 Linthorpe Road,
Middlesbrough
Wright (Frank), 100A York Road, Hartlepool

Cornwall
Bookcentre, 2 Fore Street, St Ives
Bookcentre, 23 Market Jew Street, Penzance
City Bookshop, River Street, Truro
Falmouth Bookshop, 21 Church Street, Falmouth
John Oliver, 33 Fore Street, Redruth
S.P.C.K. Bookshop, Quay Street, Truro
Spencer Thorn, Belle Vue, Bude
The Strand Bookshop, 4 The Strand, Padstow
Truro Bookshop, 18 Frances Street, Truro

Cumbria
The Art Store, 18 Main Street, Kirkby, Lonsdale
Bluebell Bookshop, Three Crowns Yard, Penrith

Book Corner, 10–14 Cavendish Street, Barrow in Furness
Cribbs Bookshop, Church Street, Whitehaven
Drings Bookshop, The Crescent, Carlisle
Duddons Books, 2 St George's Road, Millom
Greetings, 26 Lapstone Road, Millom
Fred Holdsworth, Central Buildings, Ambleside
Lakes Bookshop, Quarry Rigg, Bowness-on-Windermere
The New Bookshop, 42–44 Main Street, Cockermouth
H. Roberts, Finckle Street, Kendal
Sam Read Bookseller, Broadgate House, Grasmere
C. Thurnams, 26/32 Lonsdale Street, Carlisle

Derbyshire

Clulows, Irongate, Derby
Moorley's Bookshop, 8 Nottingham Road, Ilkeston
Narnia, Matlock Street, Bakewell

Devon

Barnstaple Bookshop, 5 Cross Street, Barnstaple
The Bookshelf, Budleigh Salterton
Bookshelf and Gallery, 20 North Street, Ashburton,
Newton Abbot
The Bookshop, 1 Brook Street, Tavistock
The Bookshop, 18 Chapel Street, Exmouth
The Bookshop, 99 High Street, Ilfracombe
The Bookshop, The Square, Barnstaple
Chapter & Verse Ltd, 38 Eastlake Walk, Drake Circus Shopping
Precinct, Plymouth
Chapter & Verse, 8 Princesshay, Exeter
Christian Literature Centre, 4 Cornwall Street, Plymouth
Condie's, 7 Heavitree Road, Exeter
Dartington Trading Company, 29 High Street, Totnes
Georges Bookshop, 146–7 Sidwell Street, Exeter
Georges Bookshop, 144 Armada Way, Plymouth
Harbour Bookshop, 12 Fairfax Place, Dartmouth
Hulland & Son, 31 High Street, Totnes
In Other Words, 38 Mannamead Road, Mutley, Plymouth

R. Mackenzie Dye, 58 Mill Street, Bideford
The Mitre Bookshop, 6 Bank Street, Newton Abbot
The Polytechnic Bookshop, 37 Mayflower Street, Plymouth
Torbooks, 286 Higher Union Street, Torquay

Dorset

Bookends, 10 Church Street, Christchurch
The Bookshop, 12 West Street, Wareham
The Dorset Bookshop Ltd, 69 East Street, Blandford Forum
Gullivers Bookshop, 28 High Street, Wimborne
Hardings, 59–61 High Street, Shaftesbury
HR & AM Harding, 8 West Street, Blandford Forum
Longmans, 4 Cornhill, Dorchester
Longmans of Bournemouth, 4 Westover Road, Bournemouth
Modern Books of Bournemouth, 347–349 Holdenhurst Road,
Bournemouth
Weymouth Bookshop, 40A St Thomas Street, Weymouth

Durham

Dressers, 26 High Row, Darlington
H. Greener, 79 Front Street, Chester-le-Street
S.P.C.K. University Bookshop, 55–57 Saddler Street, Durham

Essex

Acres of Books, Trinity Square, Woodham Ferrers
Billericay Bookshop, 7 Radford Way, Billericay
The Bookshop, 150 High Street, Loughton
Browsers Bookshop, 125 High Street, Brentwood
Burgess Bookshop, 16 Ongar Road, Brentwood
J. H. Clarke & Co Ltd, 2 Exchange Way, Chelmsford
The Colchester Bookshop, 47 Head Street, Colchester
Grindleys Bookshop, 87 Broadway, Leigh-on-Sea
Hannay, 118 High Street, Braintree
Hart's Booksellers, 5 King Street, Saffron Walden
May and Brett Ltd, 23 High Street, Dunmow
North Bookshop, North Hill, Colchester
The Pied Piper, 108 Hutton Road, Shenfield, Brentwood

Red Lion Books, 2 Red Lion Yard, Colchester
The Swan Libraries, 27 Corbets Tey Road, Upminster

Gloucestershire
Children's Bookshop, Station Road, Stroud
Colston House Bookshop, Market Place, Fairford
The Forest Bookshop, 32 Market Place, Coleford
Preedys, 88/90 Promenade, Chelmsford
Promenade Bookshop, 22 Promenade, Chelmsford
The Tewkesbury Bookshop, 93 Church Street, Tewkesbury
The Tolsey, 4 Church Street, Tetbury
Town Bookseller, Cricklade Street, Cirencester
Town Books & Toys, 15 Eastgate Street, Gloucester
Websters Bookshops Ltd, 1 The Promenade, Cheltenham

Hampshire
Baytree Bookshop Ltd, 13 The Precinct, Waterlooville
The Bookshop & Luggage Centre, 26 Station Road, New Milton
Fleet Bookshop, 245 Fleet Road, Fleet
The Fordingbridge Bookshop, 15 Salisbury Street, Fordingbridge
Hammicks Bookshop, 13 Wote Street, Basingstoke
Hammicks Bookshop, 16 Bargate, Southampton
Kings of Lymington, 105 High Street, Lymington
Moors Bookshop, 66 Bedford Place, Southampton
Page One, 2A High Street, Petersfield
Petersfield Bookshop, 16A Chapel Street, Petersfield
The Portsmouth Bookshop, 12, 14 & 16 Arundel Way,
Portsmouth
Simmonds Bookshop, 9 Union Street, Andover
Skinner & Cradock, 6 Grove Road South, Southsea
Southern Books, 4 Grosvenor Road, Aldershot
Websters Bookshops Ltd, 1/2 King's Walk, Winchester
P. & G. Wells Ltd, 11 College Street, Winchester

Hereford and Worcester
Border Books, Leominster
The Hereford Bookseller, 24 High Town, Hereford

Hereford Bookshop, 24 & 25 Church Street, Hereford
Websters Bookshops Ltd, 95 High Street, Worcester

Hertfordshire

Alban Books, Catherine Street, St Albans
Appleby, Myers & Clarke, 60 Market Street, Watford
Ann Bird Books, 56 High Street, Hemel Hempstead
The Bookworm, 25 Parliament Square, Hertford
Burgess Books, 1 Churchyard, Hitchin
Chorleywood Bookshop, 4 New Parade, Chorleywood, Rickmansworth
Copper Kettle Gallery, High Street, Much Hadham
David's Bookshop, 7 & 14 Eastcheap, Letchworth
Harpenden Books, 11 Bowers Parade, Harpenden
Hatfield Bookworm, 56 Town Centre, Hatfield
Muirs Bookshop, 198/200 High Street, Barnet
Paton Books, 34 & 32a Holywell Hill, St Albans
Recorderie, 333 Wailing Street, Radlett
Stevenage Bookshop, 7 Town Square, Stevenage
Watford Bookshop Ltd, 3 Market Street, Watford
Woods Bookshop, 115 Marlowes, Hemel Hempstead

North Humberside

Beverley Bookshop, 16 Butcher Row, Beverley
Browns of Hull, George Street, Hull
The Hallgate Bookshop, 66 Chanterlands Avenue, Hull

South Humberside

Albert Gait Ltd, 49 Friargate, Riverhead Centre, Grimsby

Kent

John Adams, 10 Angel Walk, Tonbridge
Albion Bookshop, 29 Albion Street, Broadstairs
The Albion Bookshop, 13 Mercery Lane, Canterbury
Bookcellar, 36A High Street, Whitstable
The Bookshelf, 185–187 High Street, Herne Bay
Cardy's Library Ltd, 82 High Street, Sidcup

A. P. Davis, 37 High Street, Headcorn
Goulden & Curry, 61 High Street, Tunbridge Wells
Hooks Bookshop, Westmoreland Place, Bromley
Hooks, 204 Stoneborough Centre, Maidstone
Hooks, The Green, Westerham
Magpie Bookshop, 7 The Row, New Ash Green
Pirie & Cavendar Ltd, 95 High Street, Whitstable
Sevenoaks Bookshop, 147 High Street, Sevenoaks

Lancashire
James Atkinson, 6 King Street, Ulverston
Bookshelf, 26 St Andrews Road South, St Annes
The Carnforth Bookshop Ltd, 38–42 Market Street, Carnforth
City Bookshop, 20 Common Garden Street, Lancaster
Crescent Stationers (Cleveleys) Ltd, Crescent West, Cleveleys,
Blackpool
H. Gerrard Ltd, 31 Scotland Road, Nelson
Hills Bookshop, 49 Chapel Street, Chorley
Kaydee Bookshop, 26–30 Moor Lane, Clitheroe
Lamp Community Bookshop, 22 Church Street, Leigh
Longs Booksellers Ltd, 11 Church Street, Poulton, Blackpool
Morecambe Bookshop, 48 Euston Road, Morecambe
The Scroll Bookshop, 66 Poulton Street, Kirkham
Seed & Gabbutt, 4–6 Preston New Road, Blackburn
Students' Bookshops Ltd, 20 Common Garden Street, Lancaster
Sweetens Bookshop, 48 Fishergate, Preston
J. M. Wigley, 67–71 Market Street, Lancaster

Leicestershire
Books for Children, Farndon Road, Market Harborough
Moss's Bookshop, 42 Main Street, Woodhouse Eaves,
Loughborough
Quinns Bookshop, 35 High Street, Market Harborough
Rhyme & Reason, 22 Malcolm Arcade, Silver Street, Leicester

Lincolnshire
The Coningsby Bookshop, 38 High Street, Coningsby
M. A. Copeland, 70 Southgate, Sleaford

Kays Bookshop, 24/26 South Street, Boston
Readers Rest, 13 Steep Hill, Lincoln
J. Ruddock Ltd, High Street, Lincoln
Walkers (Books) Ltd, High Street, Stamford

Greater Manchester

Alison's Books, 4 St Andrew's Court, Bolton
Books for Children Mobile Bookshop, Altrincham
Grass Roots Books, 1 Newton Street, Piccadilly
Lewis's Ltd, Market Street
E. J. Morten, 6 Warburton St, Didsbury
Norman Lucas Booksellers, 13 Ashley Road, Altrincham
Sherratt & Hughes, 17 St Annes Square
W. H. Willshaw Ltd, 16 John Dalton Street

Merseyside

The Heswall Bookshop, 5 The Mount, Heswall, Wirral
Parry Books, Bold Street, Liverpool
Russells Bookshop, 12 Brook Street, Neston, Wirral
S.P.C.K., 124 Bold Street, Liverpool

Middlesex

Barnards University Bookshop, 50 Windsor Street, Uxbridge
Corbetts Bookshop, 56 Bridge Street, Pinner
Fagins Bookshop, 297 Hale Lane, Edgware
Fagins Bookshop, 37 Church Street, Enfield
Northwood Bookshop, 46 Green Lane, Northwood
Pearsons, 15 Church Street, Enfield
Alfred Preedy & Sons Ltd, 297–301 Station Road, Harrow
Hammond Roberts, 134 Field End Road, Eastcote, Pinner
The Swan Bookshop, 12 Church Road, Teddington

West Midlands

Bookland & Co Ltd, 13/15 Litchfield Street, Wolverhampton
The Bookroom, 7 Carrs Lane, Birmingham 4
Hudson's Children's Bookshop, 116 New Street, Birmingham
J. S. Peters & Son Ltd, 28–32 Thorp Street, Birmingham
Peters Bookshops Ltd, 124 High Street, Solihull

Norfolk

The Blackhorse Bookshop, 8–10 Wensum Street, Norwich
Hungate Bookshop, 11 Princes Street, Norwich
Jarrold & Sons Ltd, London Street, Norwich
Primes Bookshop Ltd, 22 Broad Street, Kings Lynn

Northamptonshire

The Fox in the Pound Bookshop, Brixworth
Kingsthorpe Bookshop, 6–8 Harborough Road, Northampton
Towcester Bookshop, 42 Watling Street East, Towcester

Northumberland

Appleby's Bookshop, 60 Newgate Street, Morpeth

Nottinghamshire

Mushroom, 10 Heathcote Street, Nottingham
The Penguin Bookshop, 54/56 Bridlesmith Gate, Nottingham
Hudson's Bookshop, Wheeler Gate, Nottingham
The West Bridgford Bookshop, 32 Gordon Road, West Bridgford

Oxfordshire

Blackwells Children's Bookshop, 6 Broad Street, Oxford
Book House, Prama House, Summertown
Book House, 93 High Street, Thame
Children's Bookshop, Wykham Mill Farm, Banbury
The Country Bookshop, Bear Court, Burford
John (Booksellers) Ltd, Old School, First Turn,
Wolvercote, Oxford
Messrs Knight, High Street, Abingdon
Millers Bookseller, Mill Street, Wantage
The Oxford Bookseller, St Ebbes, Oxford
Red Lion Bookshop, Burford
The Witney Bookseller, 22 High Street, Witney

Salop

Bookland & Co Ltd, 22 Princes House, The Square, Shrewsbury
Children's Bookmarket, 13 Market Street, Shrewsbury

Gallery Books, 19–21 Oswald Road, Oswestry
Smallwood Lodge Bookshop, Newport

Somerset
The Dragon Bookshop, The Crescent, Taunton
Rhyme and Reason Bookshop, 34 High Street, Bridgwater
Somerton Book Centre, West Street, Somerton

Staffordshire
Bookland & Co Ltd, 19 High Street, Newcastle
Bookland & Co Ltd, 34 Princes Street, Stafford
Methodist Book Centre, Bemersley House, Gitana Street, Hanley, Stoke-on-Trent
The Old Fire Station Bookshop, Market Square, Stone
Students' Bookshop, 8 Tontine Square, Hanley, Stoke-on-Trent
Studiocraft Galleries, The Dolphin, High Street, Abbots Bromley, Rugeley
Webberley & Co Ltd, Percy Street, Hanley, Stoke-on-Trent

Suffolk
The Ancient House Bookshop, 25–27 Upper Brook Street, Ipswich
Bennett's Bookshop, 120 High Street, Newmarket
The Castle Bookshop, Framlingham, Woodbridge
The Deben Bookshop, 33 The Thoroughfare, Woodbridge
Galaxy Bookshop, 112 High Street, Hadleigh, Ipswich
Kestrel Bookshop, 10/12 Friar's Street, Sudbury
The Saxon Bookshop, 2 Hatter Street, Bury-St-Edmunds
Suffolk Bookshop, 4 Whiting Street, Bury-St-Edmunds
Woodbridge Books, 66 The Thoroughfare, Woodbridge

Surrey
Ancient House Bookshop, 51 Bell Street, Reigate
Army & Navy, High Street, Guildford
Ascots, 8 Ockham Road South, East Horsley
Baines Bookshop, 3 Lower Square, Civic Centre, Sutton
Bentalls, Clarence Street, Kingston-upon-Thames

Bookcase, 43 Old Woking Road, West Byfleet
Bookmark, 12a Anyards Road, Cobham
Book Selections, 15 Whytecliffe Road, Purley
The Bookshop, 60 High Street, Camberley
The Bookshop, 13 Station Approach, Virginia Water
The Bookshop, Cranleigh
J. P. & L. D. Burnett, 14 The Crescent, Station Road, Woldingham
Cannings, 181 High Street, New Malden
Esher Bookshop, 7 Church Street, Esher
Fountain Bookshop, 1 New Zealand Avenue, Walton-on-Thames
F. & R. Freedman, 10 High Street, Caterham
Hammicks Bookshop, 46 Downing Street, Farnham
W. & A. Houben, 2 Church Court, Richmond
The Ibis, 109 High Street, Banstead
Joyland, 56 Frimley High Street, Frimley, Camberley
Just Books, High Street, Haslemere
Lion & Unicorn, 19 King Street, Richmond
Nancy Leigh Bookshop, Chapel Street, Woking
Penguin Bookshop, 10 King Street, Richmond
Pullinger Ltd, 56 High Street, Epsom
Regency Bookshop, 45 Victoria Road, Surbiton
Samson Books, Unit 66/67, The Market Hall, High Street, Epsom
The Surrey Bookshop, 11 Kings Shade Walk, Epsom
Turners Bookshop, 46 Chipstead Valley Road, Coulsdon
Websters Bookshops Ltd, 1063/4/7 Whitgift Centre, Croydon
Websters Bookshops Ltd, 55/60 South Street, Dorking, Surrey
Websters Bookshops Ltd, 20/21 Friary Centre, Guildford
Weybridge Books, 28 Church Street, Weybridge
Whitehall Bookshop, 51 The Broadway, Cheam

East Sussex

Battle Bookshop, 24 High Street, Battle
The Cliffe Bookshop, 22 Cliffe High Street, Lewes
Harpers Bookshop, 64 Grove Road, Eastbourne
Johnson's Bookshop, 112 South Street, Eastbourne
Sally Lunn, 50 Meads Street, Eastbourne

Maltby Books, 4 The Broadway, Crowborough
Martello Bookshop, 26 High Street, Rye
The Mint House, High Street, Hurstpierpoint
Robinson's Bookshop, 11 Bond Street, Brighton
Scorpio Bookshop & Gallery, 50 High Street, Battle
Stanley Botes Bookseller Ltd, Beeching Road South, Bexhill
Websters Bookshops Ltd, 55/6 North Street, Brighton

West Sussex

Jackie Baynes, 14 Park Way, Pound Hill, Crawley
Books and Things, 60 High Street, Billingshurst
The Bookstop, 44a High Street, Lindfield
Edlows, 17 Churchill Parade, Rustington
The Halcyon Bookshop, 11 The Broadway, Haywards Heath
Hammicks Bookshop, 23 West Street, Horsham
Hooks, 16 Haslett Avenue, Crawley
Mason & Hodges Ltd, 6 Goring Road, Worthing
Midhurst Bookshop, Knockhundred Row, Midhurst
Optimus Books, 27 Warwick Street, Worthing
Wessex Bookshop, South Street, Chichester

Tyne & Wear

T. & G. Allen, 275 Whitley Road, Whitley Bay
Bible House, 14 Pilgrim Street, Newcastle-upon-Tyne
The Bookshop, 13 Ridley Place, Newcastle-upon-Tyne
Holmes McDougall Bookselling, Sandy Lane, North Gosforth, Newcastle-upon-Tyne
Mawson Swan & Morgan, Grey Street, Newcastle-upon-Tyne
The Park Bookshop, 185 Park View, Whitley Bay, Tyne & Wear
Thorn's Children's Bookshop, Eldon Square, Newcastle-upon-Tyne

Warwickshire

John Gould, The Warwick Bookshop, 9 High Street, Warwick
George Over Ltd, 16 High Street, Rugby
Leamington Bookshop, Regent Street, Leamington Spa
The Stratford Bookshop Ltd, 47 Henley Street, Stratford-upon-Avon

Wiltshire

Bruton Education Supplies Ltd, 106 Eastern Avenue, Chippenham
Everyman Bookshop, 5 Bridge Street, Salisbury
Foster's Bookshop, The High Street, Wootton Bassett, Nr Swindon
The White Horse Bookshop, 136 High Street, Marlborough

North Yorkshire

Blake Head Bookshop, 104 Micklegate, York
Castle Hill Books, 1b Castle Hill, Richmond
S. G. Hitchen Ltd (Austicks), 14 Princes Street, Harrogate
Holmans Bookshop, 19/21 Skinner Street, Whitby
The Penguin Bookshop, Coppergate, York
Pickerings, 42 The Shambles, York
St Margaret's Bookshop, 10–11 Kirkgate, Ripon
Thomas C. Godfrey Ltd, 21–25 Stonegate, York

South Yorkshire

The Barnsley Bookshop, 8 Pitt Street, Barnsley
The Broomhill Bookshop, 257 Fulwood Road, Broomhill, Sheffield
Endcliffe Bookshop, 477 Ecclesall Road, Sheffield
Hartley Seed, 154–158 West Street, Sheffield
The Methodist Bookshop, 47 Chapel Walk, Sheffield
The Pilgrim Bookshop, 17 Bradford Row, Hallgate, Doncaster
Sheffield Independent Bookshop Ltd, 341 Glossop Road, Sheffield
Wards Bookshop, 35 Chapel Walk, Sheffield

West Yorkshire

Austicks Children's Bookshop, 12 Great George Street, Leeds
W. H. Bean & Co (Leeds) Ltd, 9 Dolly Lane, Leeds
Bookmark, 2 Wenthill Close, High Ackworth, Pontefract
Broadbent, 16 The Grove, Ilkley
Children's Bookshop, 37–39 Lidget Street, Lindley, Huddersfield
Childs Play, Holme Street, Hebden Bridge

Crossgates Wonderland, Arndale Centre, Leeds
Greenhead Books, 9 Market Walk, Huddersfield
Greenhead Books, The Bond Street Shopping Centre, Leeds 1
Greenhead Books, Oldgate, Huddersfield
Huddersfield Children's Bookshop, 39 Lidget Street, Lindley, Huddersfield
The McDonald Book Co Ltd, 173 Sunbridge Road, Bradford
Stringers & Sons Ltd, Cross Green Rise, Pontefract Lane, Leeds
Walkers Bookshop, 28 Arndale Centre, Leeds
Wetherby Bookshop, 20A Bank Street, Wetherby

Channel Islands

Les Caches, St Martins, Guernsey
De Gruchy, King Street, St Helier, Jersey
The Jura Bookshop, 44 Don Street, St Helier, Jersey
L.S.T. Ltd, 9 Patriotic Street, St Helier, Jersey
Unique Bookshop, Unit 8, Springside, Trinity, St Helier, Jersey

Isle of Man

The Bridge Bookshop, The Square, Castletown
The Bridge Bookshop, Shore Road, Port Erin
St Paul's Book Centre, St Paul's Square, Ramsey

Isle of Wight

The Book Centre, High Street, Newport

Northern Ireland

Books Etc, 7 Riverdale, Larne, Co Antrim
Bookfare, 99–101 Church Street, Ballymena, Co Antrim
Camerons, Broughshane Street, Ballymena, Co Antrim
Cranes Bookshop, 37–39 Rosemary Street, Belfast 1
Eason & Son, Castle Centre, Antrim
Eason & Son, 17 Donegall Street, Belfast
Family Books, The Sabbath School Society, Fisherwick Place, Belfast
J. P. Gardener & Son Ltd, 70–72 Botanic Avenue, Belfast
North West Books, 23 Main Street, Limavady, Co Londonderry
North-West Books, 23 Bridge Street, Coleraine, Co Londonderry

University Bookshop, 91 University Road, Belfast
William Mullan & Son, 12 Donegall Place, Belfast

Republic of Ireland

Book Centre, 10 High Street, Kilkenny
Book Centre, 9 Michael Street, Waterford
Bookshop, 'Book Ends', 44 Main Street, Howth, Co Dublin
Bookstop, Dun Laoghaire Shopping Centre, Dun Laoghaire, Co Dublin
Books Unlimited, Donaghmede Shopping Centre, Dublin 13
Bray Bookshop, 15 Quinsboro Road, Bray, Co Wicklow
Day's Bazaar Ltd, 30–32 Oliver Plunkett Street, Mullingar, Co Westmeath
Dun Drum Bookshop, Main Street, Dun Drum, Dublin 14
Eason & Son, Irish Life Mall, Talbot Street, Dublin 2
Eason & Son, 40 Lower O'Connell Street, Dublin 1
Eason & Son, 5 Upper George's Street, Dun Laoghaire, Dublin
Eason & Son, 111 Patrick Street, Cork
Eason & Son, 9 O'Connell Street, Limerick
The Ennis Bookshop, 13 Abbey Street, Ennis, Co Clare
Greene & Co Ltd, 16 Clare Street, Dublin 2
Fred Hanna & Co, 28 Nassau Street, Dublin 2
Hodges Figgis, 56 Dawson Street, Dun Laoghaire, Dublin 2
International Educational Services (School & Library Suppliers), Captains Hill, Leixlip, Co Kildare
McGowans Bookshop, 4 Dublin Road, Stillorgan, Co Dublin
Nimble Fingers, Stillorgan Road, Stillorgan, Co Dublin
O'Gormans Bookshop, Shop Street, Galway
O'Mahony's Bookshop, 120 O'Connell Street, Limerick
Paperback Centre, 20 Suffolk Street, Dublin 2
The Paperback Centre, Stillorgan Shopping Centre, Stillorgan, Co Dublin
The Rathfarnham Bookshop, Shopping Centre, Rathfarnham, Dublin 16

Scotland

Bauermeister Booksellers, 19 George IV Bridge, Edinburgh
J. G. Blissett, Upper Kirkgate, Aberdeen

Blacklock Farries & Sons Ltd, Church Crescent, Dumfries
Bookpoint, 147–149 Argyll Street, Dundon, Argyll
Bookshelf, Newmarket Street, Ayr
The Bookshop, 37 Douglas Street, Milngavie, Glasgow
Bookworms, 7 East Clyde Street, Helensburgh, Dunbartonshire
Browsers, 25 High Street, Dunblane, Perthshire
Norman Burns, Bridge Street, Dunkeld, Perthshire
The Country Children's Bookshop, The Mews Arcade,
Saltoun Street, Glasgow
Church of Scotland Bookshop, Union Street, Aberdeen
Church of Scotland Bookshop, 121A George Street, Edinburgh
Church of Scotland Bookshop, 160 Buchanan Street, Glasgow
Edinburgh Bookshop, 57 George Street, Edinburgh
M. H. Ford & Son, 110 Ayr Road, Newton Mearns, Glasgow
Frasers, 21–59 Buchanan Street, Glasgow
R. Gibson & Son (Glasgow), 17 Fitzroy Place, Glasgow G3
Holmes McDougall Booksellers, Clydeholm Road, Glasgow
J. & G. Innes, 107 South Street, St Andrews, Fife
Interbrook Centre, Unit 2, Oakbank Estate, Glasgow G20
Jenners Ltd, Princes Street, Edinburgh
Kay's Bookshop, 390 Morningside Road, Edinburgh 10
McDougal Bros, 3 Moss Street, Paisley, Renfrewshire
J. R. MacGougan, 14 Ayr Street, Troon, Ayrshire
H. T. MacPherson Ltd, 24 Chalmers Street, Dunfermline, Fife
N. Melrose, Churchill, 70 Morningside Road, Edinburgh
Melvens Bookshop, 176 High Street, Perth
Melvens Bookshop, 29 Union Street, Inverness
Merry Go Round, 15 Kirk Wynd, Kirkcaldy
New Age Bookshop, 225 High Street, Kirkcaldy, Fife
The Ochil Bookshop, 10 St John's Place, Kirkside, Perth
John Smith & Son (Glasgow), 57 St Vincent Street, Glasgow G1
John Smith & Son (Glasgow) Ltd, 406 Sauchiehall Street,
Glasgow G3
James Thin, 54–56 South Bridge, Edinburgh
Thistle Bookshops Ltd, 6 Havelock Street, Glasgow G11
Thistle Bookshops Ltd, 16 West Nile Street, Glasgow
Ann R. Thomas Gallery, Tarbert, Argyll

Watt & Grant, 247 Union Street, Aberdeen
J. D. Yeadon & Co, 32 Commerce Street, Elgin, Grampian
J. Yule & Sons Ltd, 3–5 Commerce Street, Arbroath

Wales

The Bookcellar, Mitre Terrace, Pwllheli, Gwynedd
Bookland & Co Ltd, 4 Garth Road, Bangor, Gwynedd
Bookland & Co Ltd, 5 Ladywell Centre, Newtown, Powys
Bookland & Co Ltd, 9 Queen Street, Wrexham, Clwyd
The Bookshop, 42 Castle Street, Beaumaris, Gwynedd
The Bookshop, 34/36 Market Street, Haverfordwest, Dyfed
Books Unlimited, 210 High Street, Prestatyn, Clwyd
Chapter & Verse, 23–25 Morgan Arcade, Cardiff
The Cheese Press, 18 High Street, Crickhowell, Powys
City Books & Toys, 224 High Street, Bangor, Gwynedd
Clwyd Books, 89 Conway Road, Colwyn Bay, Clwyd
Clwyd Books, Harmony House, St Georges Place, Llandudno, Gwynedd
Geo Williams, Mariner Street, Swansea
Gray–Thomas, 9–11 Castle Ditch, Caernarfon, Gwynedd
Griffin Bookshop, 103A The Struet, Brecon, Powys
Lears Bookshop, 13 Royal Arcade, Cardiff
Paperback Parade, 176 Dock Street, Newport, Gwent
Uplands Bookshop, 4 Gwydr Square, Uplands, Swansea
Uplands Bookshop, 7 Union Street, Swansea
Webb & Son, Telford Place, Menai Bridge, Gwynedd
Ystwyth Books, 7 Princes Street, Aberystwyth, Dyfed

The Booksellers Association is always happy to give advice and information on where to buy books. Please telephone 01-730 8214 or write to The Booksellers Association of Great Britain and Ireland, 154 Buckingham Palace Road, London SW1.

W. H. Smith and John Menzies

Most of the larger branches of W. H. Smith & Son Ltd and John Menzies Plc carry a wide selection of children's books. Both offer

book–order services. To find out the branch in your area, please ring: W. H. Smith & Son Ltd – 01-730 1200
John Menzies Plc – 031-225 8555 Extension 3207

Commercial book clubs

There are several commercial book clubs which you can join, and these have some real advantages. In essence, they enable you to buy books for your children by mail order. When you join, the usual practice is for you to be sent information about the books on offer several times a year. You choose the books you want, order them – and they arrive by post later on.

My kids think it's great to get something through the post, especially a parcel, and most children enjoy belonging to clubs of any sort. Another major advantage of a book club is that the books are usually sold at a discount, so they actually cost less than they do in the shops.

Some people worry that by joining a book club they'll be committing themselves to buying lots of books that they don't want. It's true that when you join a book club you'll probably have to agree to buy a certain number of books in your first year. It isn't usually many, though, and there is a good reason. It's part of an agreement between publishers, booksellers and book clubs which says that new books can only be sold at a discount through a real club. To make it a club, you as a member have to agree to buy a minimum number of books in your first year.

Red House Books is a highly successful book club which now has over 100,000 families in its membership. On joining, you have to agree to buy three books in your first year. As a member, you get eight issues a year of *Red House Post*, a magazine telling you about the books on offer. It will arrive every six to eight weeks, and there's a different selection of books every time. Unlike most adult book clubs, Red House Books also offers paperbacks. You'll usually have a choice of up to fifty books.

The average discount offered is around twenty-five per cent off the publisher's price, and you should get the book you order by return of post. Red House Books also say that if you're not satisfied with a particular book, you can return it and you'll get a full refund. Books for all ages of children are offered, from babies to teenagers, but their main area is up to the age of eight, with the biggest concentration being in books for the under-fives.

Red House Books, Witney, Oxfordshire OX8 6YQ (Telephone: 0993 71144).

Books for Children is a book club which often runs special introductory offers (as does Red House Books). Such an offer might give you a lot of children's books for a very small price, and they're always worth looking out for – you'll usually find them in the advertising pages of magazines such as *Parents*.

If you join Books for Children, you'll have to commit yourself to buying four books in your first year. The club only offers hardbacks, but discounts range from twenty to fifty per cent on publishers' prices, and sometimes discounts can be even higher. As a member, you'll get a magazine thirteen times a year which not only features at least thirty books for you to choose from, but several pages of news and views devoted to children's books in general.

Books on offer are divided into four main sections, according to the age of the child for which they're suitable. These divisions are for the under-fives, the four to sevens, sevens to tens and children over ten. Books on offer in the magazine are therefore 'flagged' with an age range.

Books for Children, Park House, Dollar Street, Cirencester, Gloucestershire (Telephone: 0285 67081).

Letterbox Library is an interesting book club which is claimed to be the only one specializing in non-sexist and multi-cultural books for children. It hasn't been around for very long, but seems to be going from strength to strength. The club currently has a £2.50 joining fee, after which you have to agree to buy three books in your first year. Paperbacks are on offer as well as hardbacks, and most of the books are available at a discount.

If you don't want to buy the books, though, you can simply be a subscriber, which means you'll get a quarterly magazine and a newsletter with plenty of book information. Letterbox Library aims to offer a range of sixty or more books a year, as well as a back list of titles they've offered before. As a book club, Letterbox Library does offer a valuable service. It will help to point you in the direction of books which redress the balance in a society still dominated, to a large extent, by stereotypes of all sorts.

Letterbox Library, Children's Books Co-operative, 1st Floor, 5 Bradbury Street, London N16 8JN (Telephone: 01-254 1640).

The Good Book Guide is a combination of magazine and mail order service. The magazine features reviews of over a 1,000 adult and children's books every year as well as author interviews and other articles. Books are shown in full colour, something which makes *The Good Book Guide to Children's Books* – a once yearly special on children's books – well worth getting hold of. It's been published in conjunction with Penguin Books to date, and the current issue is available in bookshops, price £3.95. Full subscription, however, will give you a copy of *The Good Book Guide to Children's Books*, plus five colour illustrated Guides, an Annual Selection, supplements and special surveys. All books reviewed are available by mail order. At the time of writing, U.K. and Eire subscription is £9.50; Europe £11; and outside Europe, £12.50.

The Good Book Guide, PO Box 400, London SW8 4AU.

The Puffin Clubs are run by Penguin Books, whose paperbacks for children are published as Puffins. There are two clubs, the Puffin Club proper, for eight to thirteen year olds, and the Junior Puffin Club for younger readers, the four- to eight-year-old age group. Subscription to either club at present costs £2.50 per child per year, although you can get a family subscription (covering all your children) for £3. As a member, your child will receive a special Puffin Club badge, a membership book, a 28-page magazine (*The Egg* for young ones, *Puffin Post* for the over-eights) four times a year, and various other benefits. There's usually an annual Puffin exhibition and other jamboree-type events at which your child will be able to meet all sorts of celebrities and authors and generally have a good time.

The magazines are certainly worth having, too. They're usually full of stories, poems, cartoons, illustrations and articles by some of the best authors and illustrators working in children's books. The Puffin Clubs have also become a registered book club, so you can now buy books from them by mail order, some of them at reduced prices, too. Watch out for special introductory offers, and be prepared for your children to become real Puffin Club fanatics – mine are, at any rate!

The Puffin Clubs, Penguin Books Ltd, 27 Wright's Lane, London W8 5TZ. Information about Puffin Books is also available from the Puffin Marketing Department, at the same address.

Macdonald 345 isn't strictly speaking, a book club at all, although it is produced by a leading publisher of children's books. It's described by the publishers as a 'playschool through the post', and as 'a co-ordinated range of books, records, games and activities for the pre-school child to use alone or with help from a teacher'.

The idea is that you sign up for a year, and then you will receive a monthly pack of material designed to help your child develop the skills she'll need when she goes to school. The pack contains models, reading material, puzzles, pictures, records and lots more, and the emphasis is on learning through fun. Each pack also gives you plenty of ideas for games and other activities with your child. At the time of writing the whole year's course costs just £31.65 for the twelve packs, and it all comes highly recommended by various educational experts. Macdonald also publishes a range of books for the under-fives designed to tie in with the nursery course. These, too, can be obtained by mail order.

Macdonald 345, details from Purnell Ltd, Paulton, Bristol BS18 5LQ. Book details from The Marketing Department, Macdonald, Greater London House, Hampstead Road, London NW1 7QX. (Telephone: 01-377 4600).

Finding out about books

It's worth keeping your eyes open for reviews of new children's books in newspapers and magazines. They're not all that frequent, but they do pop up from time to time. In magazines like *Parents*, though, they appear regularly, and there are also occasional book related features, such as interviews with authors or coverage of major awards, like the **Parents Magazine Best Books for Babies Award**, which happens annually.

There are several specialist magazines which are well worth subscribing to if you really want to find out about children's books.

Books for Keeps is certainly the best of the bunch. It features reviews, interviews and special features on all aspects of children's books and reading. It's published by **The School Bookshop Association**, an organization which promotes the idea of having bookshops in schools and supports the thousands which are already in existence. *Books for Keeps* is published six times a year, and an annual subscription currently costs £6.60 (overseas £9.50).

The SBA also publishes several guides. *How to Set Up and Run a School Bookshop* currently costs £1.50 including postage and packing. Then there are the two guides to *Children's Books for a Multi-Cultural Society*, one focusing on books for children from birth to seven years old (£2.50, including postage and packing) and one on children aged eight to twelve (£1.75 including postage and packing). They're both excellent and do a marvellous job of collecting together information on books and organisations which counter stereotypes and promote multi-cultural understanding.

Books for Keeps, The School Bookshop Association, 1 Effingham Road, Lee, London SE12 8NZ (Telephone: 01-852-4953).

The Federation of Children's Book Groups is an organization which links the activities of book groups all over the country. Most such book groups are formed of parents and people interested in children's books, and there is probably a group in your area. Details from Acting Secretary Jan Wilde, 32 Howard Avenue, Kings Heath, Birmingham B14 7PD (Telephone: 021-444 0450).

Books for your Children is a very friendly and highly informative magazine about all aspects of children's books. It's still published by its founder, Anne Wood, who has a long track record as someone who has dedicated herself to helping get children and books together. _Books for your Children_ is definitely aimed at parents first and foremost, and features reviews of new hardbacks and paperbacks, interviews with authors and illustrators and all sorts of features. It's published three times a year, and an annual subscription currently costs £3.50, £5 overseas by surface mail, £7 by airmail.

  Books for your Children, 90 Gillhurst Road, Harborne, Birmingham 17.

British Book News Children's Books is a magazine published four times a year by **The British Council**. It, too, features news and reviews of children's books, and an annual subscription currently costs £12.50 (£15 overseas) or $21 in the USA and Canada. Contact: Iris Taylor, Basil Blackwell Ltd, 108 Cowley Road, Oxford OX4 1JF.

Organizations
The National Book League has a Centre for Children's Books which is involved in a number of activities relating to the promotion of and information about children's books. Not only does it keep various collections – such as a collection of all the books published over the last two years – it also administers major children's book awards. It's also there to help you find out about books. You can phone, write or visit the Centre, and they'll do their best to help you find the right books for your child.

  The NBL also holds exhibitions and produces a number of publications. There is the annual _Children's Books of the Year_, for example, a selection of the best books published in the year. Other publications available are _Learning to Read with Picture_

Books by Jill Bennett (an essential piece of reading for anyone interested in children's books), and a number of booklists published by Baker Book Services, the *Reading for Enjoyment Guides*. The Centre for Children's Books also stocks a range of books about children's literature, and all these publications are available by mail order.

The Centre for Children's Books, The National Book League, Book House, 45 East Hill, London SW18 2QZ (Telephone: 01-870 9055).

Booklists are also available from the following organizations.
The National Library for the Handicapped Child, Lynton House, Tavistock Square, London WC1H 9LT.
The School Library Association, Victoria House, 29–31 George Street, Oxford OX1 2AY.
Baker Books, Manfield Park, Guildford Road, Cranleigh, Surrey GU6 8NU.

Useful books

Babies Need Books by Dorothy Butler (Penguin Books). Originally published in 1980, this paperback is still essential reading for all parents. It covers in depth how your child develops and what sort of books she needs from birth to the age of five. Dorothy has followed it up with *Five to Eight* (The Bodley Head) which does the same for the age range of the title. Both books are full of common sense and insight based on a real knowledge of children and books.

The Read-Aloud Handbook by Jim Trelease (Penguin Books) This is also essential reading for all parents. It's a very forcefully argued book which puts the case for reading aloud to your child from birth almost throughout her childhood. Jim Trelease is a passionate advocate of children's books and if, after reading his book, you're not convinced of what they can do for your family, then I'd be very surprised indeed.

Reading Through Play by Carol Baker (Macdonald). Carol Baker's book is full of good ideas for all sorts of activities which will help your under five develop the skills she'll need in the process of learning to read.

Ms Muffet Fights Back by Rosemary Stones, available free from Penguin Books, address on page 115 (orders for more than ten copies by application).
This excellent guide to non-sexist books for children is certainly well worth getting hold of.

To understand your child's reading needs it's a great help to understand the way children develop in general. To this end it's worth looking at the following books: _Babyhood, Baby and Child_ and _The Parents' A–Z_, all by Penelope Leach, and all published by Penguin.

5

Recommended books

This has been the hardest section of all to write. It isn't that I don't know which books I'd like to recommend to you – the problem is that I'd like to recommend too many. Indeed, there are hundreds of wonderful books that your child shouldn't miss out on, and it's a daunting task to have to try and come up with a much smaller list of 'essential' books for the under-eights.

So what I've done is to list a few books here, all of which have been discussed during the main part of the book. But my advice is to look at this list of books as a mere starter-pack. . .they're books your child certainly shouldn't do without. Equally there are many more she will enjoy if you can find them for her.

That's why it's important to look in your bookshop, scan the shelves of your local libraries, join a book club, and find out as much as you can about children's books. Exciting new books are being published all the time, and there are plenty of old favourites still available – or being made available yet again.

For babies

Helen Oxenbury's *Baby Board Books* (Walker Books).
Where's Spot by Eric Hill (Heinemann hardback, Puffin paperback).
The Baby's Catalogue by Janet and Allan Ahlberg (Viking Kestrel hardback, Puffin paperback).
Round and Round the Garden by Sarah Williams and Ian Beck (Oxford University Press, hardback and paperback).
Mother Goose by Raymond Briggs (Puffin paperback).

For toddlers

Peepo! by Janet and Allan Ahlberg (Viking Kestrel hardback,

Puffin paperback).

The Shirley Hughes Nursery Collection: Bathwater's Hot, Noisy, When We Went to the Park, All Shapes and Sizes, Colours, Two Shoes New Shoes (Walker Books).

Mr Gumpy's Outing (and *Mr Gumpy's Motor Car*) by John Burningham (Jonathan Cape hardback, Puffin paperback).

In The Night Kitchen by Maurice Sendak (Puffin paperback).

A is for Angry by Sandra Bonyton (Methuen).

For pre-schoolers

Burglar Bill by Janet and Allan Ahlberg (Heinemann hardback, Fontana paperback).

The *Lucy and Tom* books, and the *Alfie* books, by Shirley Hughes (Gollancz and The Bodley Head hardbacks, Puffin and Fontana paperbacks).

Dogger by Shirley Hughes (Fontana paperback).

My Naughty Little Sister stories (Puffin paperback, some individual stories in Magnet paperbacks).

For beginner readers

The *Happy Families* series by Allan Ahlberg and various illustrators (Viking Kestrel hardbacks, Puffin paperbacks, 12 titles).

Fairy Tales by Terry Jones (Pavilion hardback, Puffin paperback).

Please Mrs Butler by Allan Ahlberg (Viking Kestrel hardback, Puffin paperback).

Here Comes Charlie Moon and *Charlie Moon and the Big Bonanza Bust-Up* by Shirley Hughes (Bodley Head hardbacks, Fontana paperbacks).

Flat Stanley by Jeff Baxter (Methuen hardback, Magnet paperback).

But remember – don't stop with these! There's plenty more brilliant books where they came from!

Books mentioned in the text

Cinderella, Jeffers/Ehrlich (Hamish Hamilton)
Topsy and Tim books, Adamson (Blackie)
Mr Magnolia, Blake (Cape and Fontana)
Willy The Wimp, Browne (Julia MacRae)
Helen Oxenbury *Baby Board Books* (Walker)
Jollypops, Colin and Jacqui Hawkins (Viking Kestrel)
Spot books, Hill (Heinemann and Puffin)
The Most Amazing Hide-and-Seek Alphabet and Counting Books,
Crowther, (Viking Kestrel)
The Baby's Catalogue, Ahlberg (Viking Kestrel and Puffin)
Round and Round the Garden, Beck/Williams (OUP)
The Mother Goose Treasury, Briggs (Hamish Hamilton and Puffin)
Mother Goose, de Paola (Methuen)
This Little Puffin, Matterson (Viking Kestrel and Puffin)
I Want to See The Moon, Baum/Daly (Bodley Head and Magnet)
Peepo!, Ahlberg (Viking Kestrel and Puffin)
Mr Gumpy's Outing and *Mr Gumpy's Motor Car*, Burningham
(Cape and Puffin)
The Elephant and the Bad Baby, Briggs/Vipont (Hamish Hamilton
and Puffin)
Where the Wild Things Are, Sendak (Puffin)
Shirley Hughes *Nursery Collection* (Walker)
Dick Bruna books (Methuen)
Lucy and Tom books, Hughes (Gollancz and Puffin)
Alfie books, Hughes (Bodley Head and Fontana)
Oh Lewis, Rice (Puffin)
Goodnight, Goodnight, Rice (Puffin)
The Bad Babies' Counting Book, Bradman/van der Beek
(Piccadilly)

A is for Angry, Boynton (Methuen)
Dogger, Hughes (Fontana)
Helpers, Hughes (Fontana)
Moving Molly, Hughes (Fontana)
Sally's Secret, Hughes (Puffin)
The Tale of Peter Rabbit, Potter (Warne)
The Seven Wild Washerwomen, Yeoman/Blake (Puffin)
Burglar Bill, Ahlberg (Heinemann and Fontana)
Funnybones, Ahlberg (Heinemann and Fontana)
My Naughty Little Sister stories, Edwards (Methuen)
Althea Books (Dinosaur)
The Twelve Dancing Princesses, Le Cain (Puffin)
Mrs Fox's Wedding, Le Cain (Puffin)
The Fairy Tale Treasury, Haviland/Briggs (Puffin)
The Helen Oxenbury Book of Nursery Stories (Walker)
Robot, Pienkowski (Heinemann)
Haunted House, Pienkowski (Heinemann)
Tiny Tim, Bennett/Oxenbury (Heinemann and Fontana)
Roger Was a Razor Fish, Bennett/Roffey (Bodley Head)
A Child's Book of Manners, Maschler/Oxenbury (Puffin)
Beginner Books (Collins)
Happy Families, Ahlberg, and various artists, 12 titles (Viking Kestrel and Puffin)
Fairy Tales, Jones (Pavilion and Puffin)
Seasons of Splendour, Jaffrey (Pavilion)
Charlie and the Chocolate Factory, Dahl (Allen & Unwin and Puffin)
The Twits, Dahl (Cape and Puffin)
The BFG, Dahl (Cape and Puffin)
Rabbiting On, Wright (Fontana)
Hot Dog, Wright (Viking Kestrel and Puffin)
Please Mrs Butler, Ahlberg (Viking Kestrel and Puffin)
The Great Smile Robbery, McGough (Viking Kestrel and Puffin)
I'm Trying To Tell You, Ashley (Viking Kestrel and Puffin)
Linda's Lie, Ashley (Julia MacRae and Puffin)
Flat Stanley, Baxter (Methuen and Magnet)
Here Comes Charlie Moon and *Charlie Moon and The Big Bonanza Bust-Up*, Hughes (Bodley Head and Fontana)

Chips and Jessie, Hughes (Bodley Head)
In The Night Kitchen, Sendak (Puffin)
Gorilla, Browne (Julia MacRae and Magnet)
Not Now Bernard, McKee (Andersen)

Index